sensual knits

FOR THE "PURE KNITTERS,"
WHO MAKE EVERY DAY
SURROUNDED BY YARN
SEEM SANE

Library of Congress Cataloging-in-Publication Data Available

10 9 8 7 6 5 4 3 2

Produced by Hollan Publishing, Inc.
100 Cummings Center, Suite 125G
Beverly, MA 01915

Published by Sterling Publishing Co., Inc.
387 Park Avenue South, New York, NY 10016

Distributed in Canada by Sterling Publishing
c/o Canadian Manda Group, 165 Dufferin Street
Toronto, Ontario, Canada M6K 3H6

Distributed in the United Kingdom by GMC Distribution Services
Castle Place, 166 High Street,
Lewes, East Sussex, England BN7 1XU

Distributed in Australia by Capricorn Link (Australia) Pty. Ltd.
P.O. Box 704, Windsor, NSW 2756, Australia

Printed in China

Sterling ISBN-13: 978-1-4027-4920-9
ISBN-10: 1-4027-4920-1

For information about custom editions, special sales, premium and corporate purchases, please contact Sterling Special Sales Department at 800-805-5489 or specialsales@sterlingpub.com.

PHOTOGRAPHY BY ALLAN PENN

COVER AND INTERIOR DESIGN BY KARLA BAKER

KNITS ILLUSTRATIONS BY KARA GOTT

sensual knits

LUXURIOUS YARNS, ALLURING DESIGNS

yahaira ferreira

An imprint of Sterling Publishing Co., Inc.

New York / London
www.sterlingpublishing.com

[CONTENTS]

INTRODUCTION

Anyone who knows me or my store knows that I have a passion for luxury fibers. It's an obsession, really, which is why my home is filled to the brim with my extravagant yarn "collection," much to the chagrin of its other inhabitant. It started simply enough one winter on a whim when I begged my future mother-in-law to teach me how to knit. When I was handed a pair of brightly colored metal needles and some squeaky acrylic yarn, it felt as if I had entered a new world. Sure, the subtleties of tension were lost on me, but there was something rhythmic and soothing about the motions. Watching that first scarf ebb and flow until finding its even ground was intoxicating.

Without knowing much about what yarns were hot or in demand, I looked around a yarn store one day and gravitated towards a fingering weight, hand-dyed merino in luscious colors. I rushed home to wind the hanks and quickly had my first "FO" (finished object). Years later, that long scarf is still worn when the temperatures drop.

Armed with the knowledge that I could create a custom piece, couture if you will, with two sticks and some wool, I pored over patterns and fashion magazines looking for the "perfect sweater." (It's the one that we have in our mind's eye but is sorely missing from our drawers.) There were obstacles keeping me from my dream knit; the patterns I ran into were lacking in the shaping or styling for which I looked; others were downright boring (this was just before the big knitting

boom). Time was another factor. As a photography student working on a thesis, knitting time was scarce and mostly snuck in between prints or on rare weekends away from the darkroom. Those cherished moments had to be enjoyable, ripping and reworking notwithstanding. I made a conscious decision to buy the best yarns I could afford. This is an easy and important step you can take: budgeting and buying for one project at a time. In doing so, you set yourself up to succeed.

The yarns I chose for this book are some of my favorites. Like the patterns themselves, they are classic without being boring. The blend of the fibers, the way they're plied, and even the rich colors they come in keep them modern and fresh. With proper care, they will last a lifetime. The silks, merinos, and cashmeres used in these decidedly sensual designs will feel soft and light against the skin while keeping you warm. But *sensual* isn't just about heavenly fabrics, it's also a state of mind. You won't want to take these pieces off. The moment you finish a project of this quality and put it on for the first time is magical. As the piece skims the body, you feel confident and eager to show off the work and the figure underneath. With their body-conscious silhouettes and creative blend of fashion-forward and classic detailing, every piece from this collection will make you feel sexy—be it a textured jacket with a nipped-in waist or a bishop-sleeve sweater with a plunging back. The juxtapositions are timeless and fresh.

This book is dedicated to the modern knitter who would rather spend her time on a one-of-a-kind look than an everyday garment. In a perfectly sensual world, fiber and needles are not drudgery but an escape.

LUXURY FIBERS

My mother always said I had expensive tastes without even knowing it. My horoscope once stated that I fall in love quickly. Combine these two traits and you end up with a stash full of luxury fibers that could fetch me the new "it bag." What can I say? I love the feel of natural yarn running through my fingers. Just as in cooking, the ingredients are the first step to a perfect finish.

ALPACA

Using alpaca guarantees a plush knit. Alpaca yarn is often softer and warmer than merino wool, with a fluid, relaxed drape. The fibers are hollow at the center, trapping air and providing an insulating effect. On crisp fall or spring days I wear my favorite short-sleeve alpaca shrug over tanks—the weight and style are perfect to keep me warm. Alpaca is known for being hypoallergenic, but don't miss the exceptional blends with other fibers, such as silk, cashmere, and merino.

ANGORA

When I think of angora, my first thought is of the ubiquitous '50s sweater girl. Angora is perfect for a sexy knit with its exceptionally soft and silky fur. However, 100 percent angora can be pricey, too warm, and sometimes sheds a lot unless combined with a more resilient fiber such as silk, wool, or alpaca. Use a pure angora for detailing, or a blend for a beautiful shawl or scarf. A trick for knitting with angora I learned from reading one of Clara Parkes's (of *Knitter's Review*) articles is to "shock" the fiber: Submerge a hank of yarn into very hot water, then cold water, and repeat a few times more before hitting the skein of yarn against a hard surface. The fibers will "both bloom and more firmly adhere to one another." If the yarn is already in a ball, try to do this as gently as possible with your finished knitted fabric.

BAMBOO

In recent years, yarn producers are looking to alternatives, such as plant-based fibers, and in the process are turning once-exotic fibers into mainstream ones. Bamboo fiber, a renewable resource, has sheen and drape similar to silk, yet feels deliciously lightweight against the skin—perfect for warm-weather wear. Bamboo yarns have gorgeous stitch definition and some compare it to linen in its strength because of its longer fiber staple. Just like silk, bamboo drinks up dye to create vibrant colors! When I don't want the weight of silk but I still want my project to dazzle, I reach for bamboo to make camisoles, light cardigans, or even wraps.

CASHMERE

Cashmere is the champagne of the yarn world. Most of the world's cashmere is plucked or shed from the soft undercoats of Mongolian and Chinese goats and the best yarn is milled in Italy or Japan. In my dream world, my stash would be stocked with champagne and only champagne. It is the softest, lightest, and warmest animal fiber around. Anticipating how soft and stunning my project will be after washing is part of the fun. Of course, in my dream world a budget is of no concern. In reality though, I save cashmere for special projects in which I want to indulge, or I'll treat myself to one skein to make a hat or scarf. Cashmere is often blended with merino and/or silk to create a lofty yarn with a gorgeous sheen at a lower price.

MERINO

Merino, my first love, is generally considered the finest and softest widely available wool fiber. If I'm not splurging on cashmere, I'm buying up merino—what I consider the bread and butter of knitting. It has a distinctive bounce and elasticity that makes it perfect for beginners. Available in all weights and colors, merino surely will be your go-to fiber. To tempt you further, there are hand-dyers creating exciting color lines ranging from subtle solids to ingenious variegations.

MOHAIR

Mohair, which also originates from goat hair, is strong and thin by nature. Commercially available mohair ranges from bulky and relatively hairy to gossamer-weight fluff. The softest mohair comes from goats less than 18 months old. It's typically labeled "Kid Mohair." While it's possible to find 100 percent mohair yarns, more commonly mohair is blended or spun with wool, silk, or other fibers to combine the shine and halo of the mohair while giving the yarn some body or thickness with the other fiber.

SILK

The drape and sheen of silk exudes glamour and luxury. Colors are always vibrant and breathtaking. Silk is both strong and soft, and warm and cool. Its lack of elasticity can make it hard to maintain an even tension. I love using silk in lace or in special projects; just remember to swatch with smaller needles than stated on the yarn label to combat stretching. Silk blends provide the sheen of silk with the elasticity of wool and may be a better bet for warmer climates or stockinette projects.

CARING AND KNITTING

Perhaps it's the photographer in me, the year of working with the archives of a library, or because I majored in anthropology, but I'm obsessed with caring for my knits. Instead of waiting until the end of the cold season to wash all my knits, I wash them when necessary. Never store a dirty sweater: There's probably some unnoticed debris that could attract moths to feast.

CARING FOR YOUR LUXURIES

There seems to be some general confusion regarding the differences between blocking and washing; however, I make no distinction between the two. "Blocking" is washing your project in pieces (sometimes) and pinning to size. "Washing" is washing your project in one piece and retaining its original size.

This is the way *I* like to wash my sweaters, which scares some people off, although I'm assuming you are dressing your swatches in mostly the same way. Measure your sweater before washing, so you know how to set it while drying. Fill a basin with lukewarm to hot water; the hot water helps degrease the fiber. Don't agitate or move the sweater—this causes fulling. Pour in a small amount of soap after your basin is full. (I used to use Synthrapol, a washing agent, but I recently switched to a no-rinse wool wash for a quicker process.) You can also use liquid dishwashing detergents. Gingerly submerge your project in the water and squeeze it a bit until it absorbs the water. Let it soak for half an hour or more, then drain. Rinse in fresh water (of the same temperature) if necessary, but never pour water directly on the sweater. You may need to repeat rinse once or twice to remove all the soap.

Squeeze the excess water out with your hands and, while supporting its weight, transfer the piece to a clean, dry towel. Roll the towel and extract more water by standing or leaning on the towel. Now take the sweater and lay flat on a drying rack or blocking board and shape or pin to your measurements. Once the sweater is completely dry, gently fold it and store it in your dresser. I like to use acid-free tissue between sweaters. If you want to keep them in your closet, buy a few acid-free boxes to store them in. I've never used mothballs or cedar and haven't had any problems yet.

THE SIZE ISSUE AND WORKING FROM A PATTERN

One of the problems I had when I first started knitting was figuring out what size to knit, the elusive idea of ease having escaped me. I always came to the question, "What size was I *supposed* to knit?" instead of "What size was *right* for me?" (a subtle but real difference). The only help I could find told me to measure my favorite sweater and follow those dimensions. Unfortunately for me, I didn't have a holy grail of sweaters. Sure, I had sweaters, but I didn't want everything I knit to be a shrunken cardigan or a not-so-perfect sweater. Going blindly into my first sweater project, I chose a pattern worked with a bulky yarn and a size that was perhaps the right one for me. Why wasn't I sure? The pattern had finished measurements and a schematic, but no suggested sizes or ease beyond a heading of S, M, L. With three sizes to choose from and no idea what kind of body or look the design was for, all I could do was guess. Needless to say, after finishing a few pieces the project was relegated to the bottom of my basket, only to be "frogged" years later.

Since then, I've figured out that bulky oversized knits don't work for me. I'd rather have my sweaters follow a closer, more slimming silhouette. The patterns in this book have a modern, close fit, ranging from negative to two to three inches of ease. When sizing is crucial, schematics are included along with finished measurements, suggested sizes to fit, and the size of the sample shown. With this information in hand, you'll be able to discern how much ease the designer built in along with what ease *you* choose.

In essence, a pattern is merely a suggestion supported by mathematical calculations. You can follow it to the letter or tinker with it here and there to get the result that's perfect for you. Want a looser fit? Knit a larger size for a different look. If the size you'd like isn't given, figure out what finished measurements you'd like. Use your gauge to recalculate your stitch count and simply use the pattern as a guide. Before you can do this, though, you need to know your body measurements. Take a tape measure and measure your chest, back, waist, arms, and so on. Write them out, draw out a skeleton chart (basically a schematic of your body), and you've created the perfect template. You can now use this to compare to all the measurements in your favorite pattern and confidently choose the size or sizes to follow. Draw the sweater schematic over your chart to catch a glimpse of how it will fit.

BODY FORM SCHEMATICS

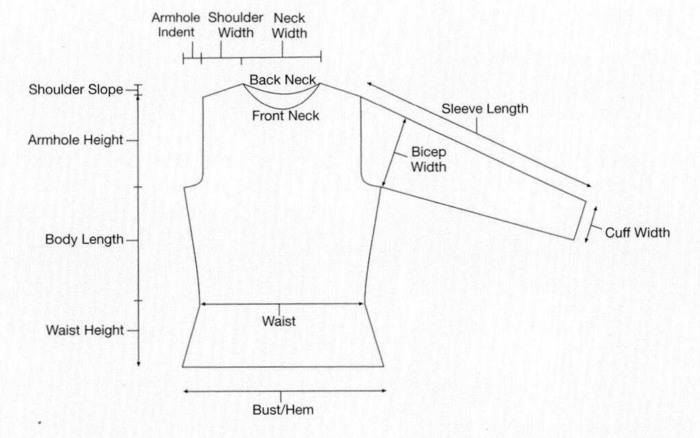

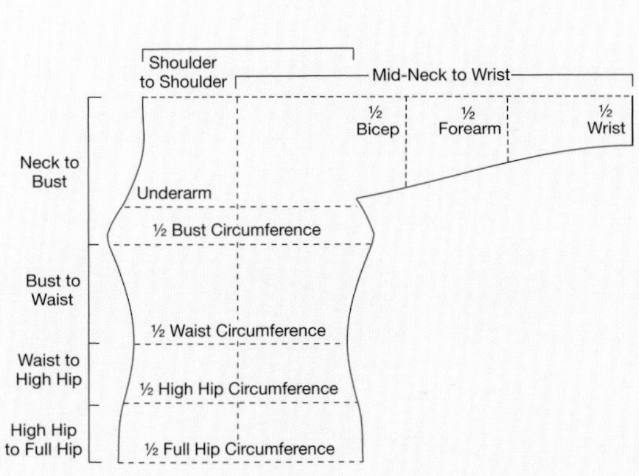

CHAPTER ONE

BARELY THERE

camisoles, light as a feather

vixen CAMISOLE

illanna weiner

This lace camisole features a unique drop stitch motif, which shows off the beautiful hand-dyed yarn. The length is easy to modify; you can turn the sexy camisole into a flattering tunic or even a sexy dress. Lightweight merino wool yarn creates a fabric with elegant drape. Layer this garment over your favorite tank top, or wear it on its own for a hot night in.

SIZES

XXS (XS, S, M, L, XL, 2X, 3X)

30–31 (32–33, 34–35, 36–37, 38–39, 40–41, 43–44, 45–46)"

Shown in size XXS

FINISHED MEASUREMENTS

unstretched

CHEST: 28 (30, 32, 34½, 36½, 38¾, 41, 43)"

LENGTH: 21 (22, 23, 24, 25, 26, 27, 28)"

YARN

YARN A: Yarntini Merino Sock (100% superwash merino wool; 430 yards/100g): 1 (2, 2, 2, 2, 2, 2, 3) skeins, Merlot

YARN B: Yarntini Merino Chunky (100% merino wool; 115 yards/100g): 1 skein, Merlot

NEEDLES

3.75mm circulars, 16 or 24" long

5mm circulars, 16 or 24" long

NOTIONS

Tapestry needle

Sewing needle or sewing machine

Sewing thread to match yarn

Two yards of store-bought lace or ribbon trim to match yarn

GAUGE

27 sts and 30 rows = 4" in lace patt before dropping sts, with Yarn A and smaller needles

17 sts and 30 rows = 4" in lace patt after dropping sts and blocking, with Yarn A and smaller needles

16 sts and 20 rows = 4" in k2, p2 rib with Yarn B and larger needles

pattern notes

The lace pattern in this camisole is very stretchy. For a sexy, tight fit, make a size 2 to 3 inches smaller than your actual bust measurement.

Find the length of circular needle that is most comfortable for you. For the smaller sizes it will probably be 16 inches; for the larger sizes it might be 24 inches.

The camisole will look very small until you drop the stitches. If you are worried about fit, make a gauge swatch, drop the stitches, block the swatch, and then measure.

The purl stitch in the center of the lace pattern will be dropped off the needle when you change to Yarn B. Don't be scared to drop the stitch—it is part of the design and will not cause the other stitches to unravel.

Illanna is a knitting fiend. Born and raised in Queens, New York, she now lives in Tempe, Arizona, where she designs and knits warm-weather garments and accessories. This multitalented knitter also enjoys sewing, beading, and cooking delicious meals. Visit her knitting blog: knitpowerstopeace.blogspot.com.

STITCH PATTERN

(Knit in the rnd)

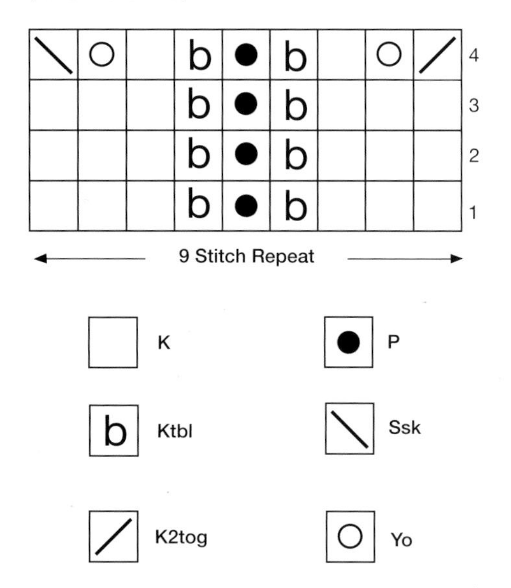

BODY

Using long-tail cast-on, Yarn A, and 3.75mm needles, CO 117 (126, 135, 144, 153, 162, 171, 180) sts. Join for working in the rnd, being careful not to twist, and pm.

Beg 9-st patt repeat, working in the rnd. Cont in patt until piece measures 18 (19, 20, 21, 22, 23, 24, 25)" from cast-on edge, or 3" less than desired length, ending with Row 1, 2, or 3 of patt.

Join Yarn B and switch to larger needle. Knit 1 rnd, dropping purl sts off LH needle. Next rnd: K1, *(p2, k2); repeat from * to last 3 sts, end p2, k1. This establishes k2, p2 rib. Work in rib for 3". BO in patt.

FINISHING

Block the camisole severely, mostly widthwise, to match schematic or desired measurements.

Try on camisole and pin store-bought lace strip into place on front and back. Alternatively, lay the camisole over a similar top that fits you to match strap positioning and length. Cut lace to desired length, adding a 2" selvage on both sides. Hand stitch or machine sew strap inside top edges of garment using either Yarn A or coordinating thread.

Weave in ends after blocking, because the garment will stretch during the blocking process.

VIXEN SCHEMATIC

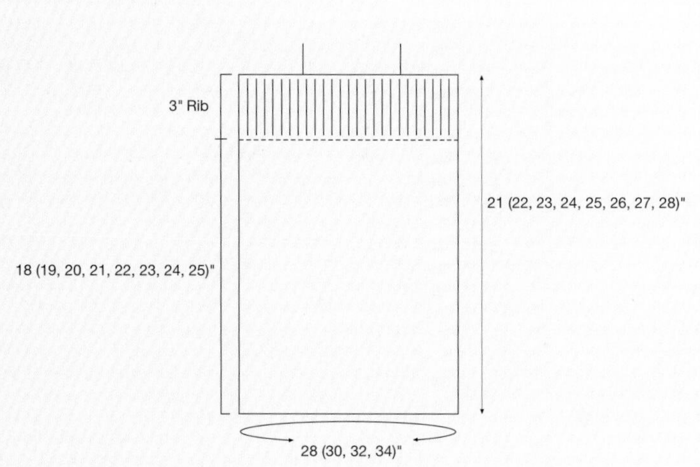

demeter CAMISOLE

miriam l. felton

This deceptively simple camisole hides a sexy little secret. The sweetheart neckline gives a hint, but the low scooped back screams "siren." Wear it under a suit jacket to add interest, or pair it with something slinky for a night out on the town. With feminine details and simple construction, this will be a knit to reach for again and again.

SIZES

XS (S, M, L, XL, 2X)

32 (36, 40, 44, 48, 52)"

Shown in size S

FINISHED MEASUREMENTS

unstretched

CHEST: 32 (36, 40, 44, 48, 52)"

WAIST: 24 (28, 32, 36, 42, 46)"

SHOULDER TO BOTTOM OF LACE: 22¼ (23½, 24½, 25¾, 27, 28)"

YARN

ShuibuiKnits (100% superwash merino wool; 191 yards/50g): 5 (5, 6, 6, 7, 7) skeins, Emerald

NEEDLES

3.5mm circular, 24" or 30" long

NOTIONS

Stitch holders or scrap yarn for holding stitches

Stitch markers

Blocking pins

GAUGE

23 sts and 36 rows = 4" in St st

pattern notes

The body begins with a provisional cast-on and is knit in the round from bottom edge to bind off for back, then worked flat. The provisional cast-on stitches are then picked up, and lace edging is knit onto bottom of camisole at a right angle, simultaneously binding off body stitches and creating the border.

When slipping stitches at the beginning of a row, slip knit stitches with yarn in back and purl stitches with yarn in front.

Miriam lives with her long-suffering husband and cat in Salt Lake City. She has had patterns published by Knit Picks, Interweave Knits, *and runs her own self-publishing business. You can find more lace and historically inspired knits at her web site, www.mimknits.com and tutorials and discussion on knitting on her blog at www.mimknits.com/wordpress.*

STITCH PATTERN

LACE EDGING

- RS: K / WS: P
- RS: K2tog / WS: P2tog
- No Stitch
- RS: P / WS: K
- RS: P2tog / WS: K2tog
- RS: Slip stitch as if to purl, wyib / WS: Slip stitch as if to purl, wyif
- RS: Ssk / WS: P2tog tbl
- Yo

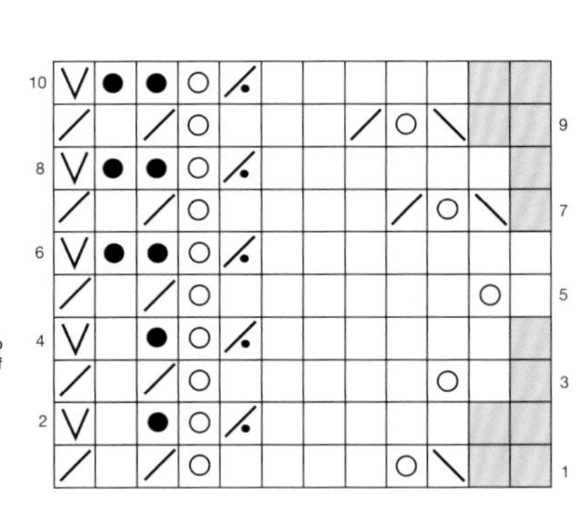

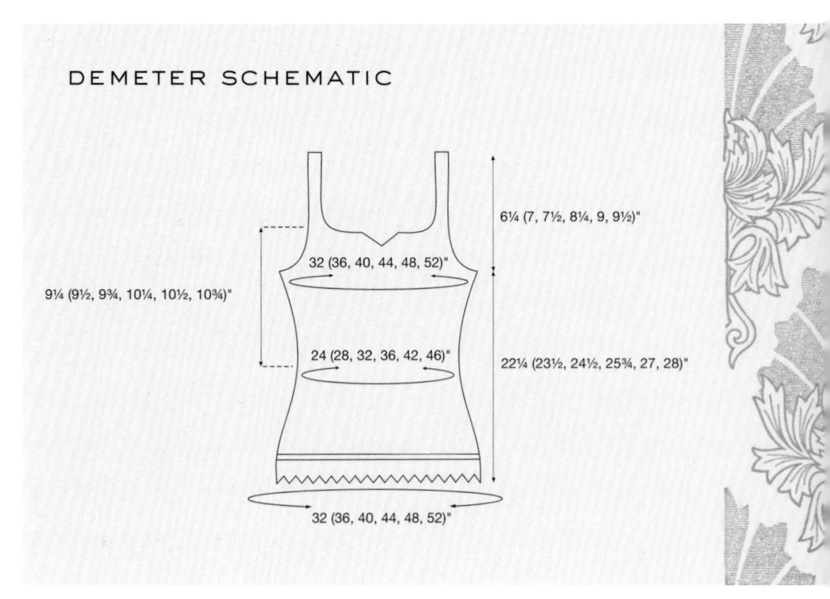

BODY

MAIN BODY IN THE RND

Provisionally cast on 180 (200, 220, 250, 280, 300) sts and join for working in the rnd being careful not to twist. Pm at beg of rnd.

Knit even for 2 (4, 6, 6, 8, 10) rnds, placing 2nd marker after 90 (100, 110, 125, 140, 150) sts.

DEC RND: *K1, k2tog, knit to 3 sts before marker, ssk, k1, sm; rep from * to 2nd marker.

Knit even for 4 rnds.

Repeat last 5 rnds 9 more times; 140 (160, 180, 210, 240, 260) sts rem.

INC RND: *K1, m1, knit to 1 st before marker, m1, k1, sm; rep from * to 2nd marker.

Knit even for 6 (6, 6, 6, 7, 7) rnds.

Rep last 7 (7, 7, 7, 8, 8) rnds 9 more times.

Work 0 (2, 4, 8, 0, 4) rnds even—70 (72, 74, 78, 80, 84) rows worked from first waist increase, and 180 (200, 220, 250, 280, 300) sts total.

K30 (30, 30, 37, 37, 37) sts, p30 (40, 50, 51, 66, 76) sts, knit to end of rnd.

K30 (30, 30, 37, 37, 37) sts, BO (in purl) 30 (40, 50, 51, 66, 76) sts for back neck, k1, ssk, knit to end of rnd.

K26 (26, 26, 33, 33, 33) sts k2tog, k2, turn work and beg working flat.

BACK BODY AND ARMHOLES

FLAT BODY

ROWS 1, 3, 5, 7 (WS): Sl 2 wyif, p2tog, purl to last 4 sts, p2togtbl, p2.

ROW 2 (RS): Sl 2 wyib, ssk, k to last 4 sts, k2tog, k2.

ROW 4, 6: Sl 2, knit to end.

WORK ARMHOLES

NEXT (RS) ROW: Sl 2, knit to 9 (9, 9, 16, 16, 16) sts before marker, BO 18 (18, 18, 32, 32, 32) sts for left armhole, knit to 9 (9, 9, 16, 16, 16) sts before next marker, BO 18 (18, 18, 32, 32, 32) sts for right armhole, knit to end of row.

BACK RIGHT STRAP

Sl 2, purl to last 4 sts, p2tog tbl, p2.

Sl 2, knit to end.

Rep last 2 rows 3 more times—10 sts rem. Cont in St st, slipping first 2 sts as established until strap measures 6¼ (7, 7½, 8¼, 9, 9½)" from armhole bind-off or desired length to shoulder. BO back right strap sts.

BACK LEFT STRAP

With WS facing, attach yarn and work as for right strap, reversing shaping and using p2tog for decs.

FRONT AND FRONT STRAPS

FRONT

Sl 2, p2tog, purl to last 4 sts, p2tog tbl, p2.

Sl 2, knit to end.

Rep these 2 rows 3 (3, 3, 2, 3, 3) more times.

SIZE L ONLY:

Sl 2, p2tog, purl to last 4 sts, p2tog tbl, p2.

Sl 2, k47, ssk, knit to end.

Sl 2, purl to end.

DIVIDE FOR NECKLINE

Sl 2, k30 (35, 40, 47, 48, 53) (center front), place rem unworked sts on st holder or scrap yarn, and turn to work left front—32 (37, 42, 49, 50, 55) sts.

LEFT FRONT

Sl 2, p2tog, purl to end.

Sl 2, knit to end.

Rep last 2 rows 3 times.

Sl 2, p2tog, knit to last 12 sts, p12.

Sl 2, k10, purl to last 2 sts, k2.

BO in knit until 12 sts rem, sl 1, p2tog, purl to end.

Sl 2, knit to end.

Sl 2, p2tog, purl to end.

Cont as for back strap. BO all sts.

RIGHT FRONT

With RS facing, attach yarn at center front neck edge.

Knit 1 row. Complete as for left front, reversing all shaping and using p2tog tbl for decs.

LACE EDGING

Return all sts from provisional cast-on to needle.

CO 10 additional sts so they sit right before provisional cast-on sts.

Begin working lace patt as charted, knitting the last st on each RS row together with 1 st from provisional cast-on.

Rep 10-row patt 36 (40, 44, 50, 56, 60) times, until all body sts are bound off. BO final 9 sts of lace.

FINISHING

Seam beg of lace band to end of lace band. Sew straps at shoulders, being careful not to twist. Weave in all ends. Block lightly to finished measurements, pinning out each point of lace.

pink sundae CAMISOLE

patrizia steadman

A delicate looking camisole that shows off your sweet side with details such as lace and picot edging, while it oozes feminity with a form-fitting style and bare shoulders. Knit in a plush merino for next-to-skin softness, it is the perfect top to wear on cool spring days or early fall nights when a little warmth is needed.

SIZES

XS (S, M, L, XL)

30–31 (32–33, 34–35, 36–37, 38–39)"

Shown in size M

FINISHED MEASUREMENTS

CHEST: 28 (30, 32, 34, 36)"

LENGTH: 13½" for all sizes, excluding I-cord straps

YARN

Pear Tree 4-ply Merino (100% Australian Merino; 175 yards/50g): 3 (3, 3, 4, 4) skeins, Blush

NEEDLES

2.75mm circulars, 24" or 32" long

3mm circulars, 24" or 32" long

2.75mm dpns

NOTIONS

Stitch markers, including one in contrasting color

Four ¼" (5mm) shank buttons

Scrap yarn

GAUGE

31 sts and 45 rows = 4" in St st

pattern notes

It may be helpful to use a contrasting marker for beginning of round (center back) to distinguish it from other markers.

If markers interfere with increases/decreases, remove them when working stitches and then replace them.

Use a larger needle when binding off Wavy Border, as this pattern creates a less stretchy fabric than the rest of the body.

Patrizia has been knitting for eighteen years and has recently started writing patterns when not recycling yarn from thrift store finds. She has been known to get a buzz from a great bargain and violently rip a store-bought sweater or two. Visit her site: ziaperamore.blogspot.com.

STITCH PATTERNS

ENGLISH MESH LACE

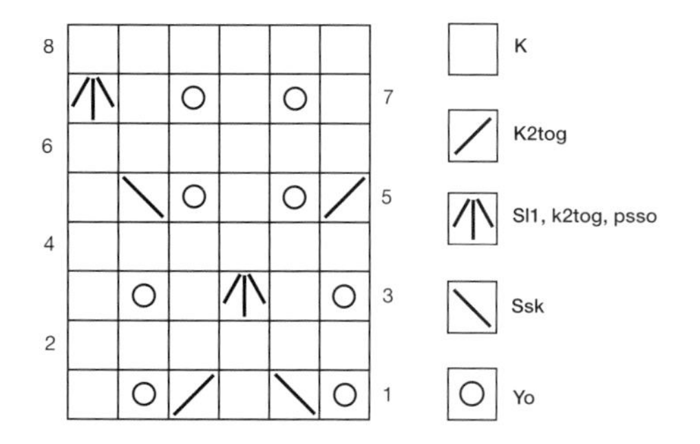

(multiple of 6 sts; 8-rnd repeat)

RND 1: *Yo, ssk, k1, k2tog, yo, k1; rep from* around.

RND 2 AND ALL EVEN RNDS: Knit.

RND 3: *Yo, k1, sl1-k2tog-psso, k1, yo, k1; rep from * around.

RND 5: *K2tog, yo, k1, yo, ssk, k1; rep from * around.

RND 7: K2, yo, k1, yo, k1, sl1-k2tog-psso, *(k1, yo, k1, yo, k1, sl1-k2tog-psso); rep from * to last 5 sts, k1, yo, k1, yo, k1.

WAVY BORDER

(21 sts, 14-rnd repeat)

ROW 1: K12, yo, k5, yo, k2tog, yo, k2.

ROW 2: K2, p11, k2, p to end.

ROW 3: K13, sl 1, k2tog, psso, k2, (yo k2tog) twice, k1.

ROW 4: K2, p9, k2, p to end.

ROW 5: K12, sl 1, k1, psso, k2, (yo, k2tog) twice, k1.

ROW 6: K2, p8, k2, p to end.

ROW 7: K11, sl 1, k1, psso, k2, (yo, k2tog), twice, k1.

ROW 8: K2, p7, k2, p to end.

ROW 9: K10, sl 1, k1, psso, k2, (yo, k2tog) twice, k1.

ROW 10: K2, p6, k2, p to end.

ROW 11: K9, sl 1, k1, psso, k2, yo, k1, yo, k2tog, yo, k2.

ROW 12: K2, p7, k2, p to end.

ROW 13: K9, (k3, yo) twice, k2tog, yo, k2.

ROW 14: K2, p9, k2, p to end.

MOSS STITCH

(multiple of 2 sts plus 1)

*P1, k1; rep from * to last st, p1.

Repeat on all rows.

BODY

HEM

Using provisional cast-on and 2.75mm circular needles, CO 198 (210, 222, 234, 246) sts. Join for working in the rnd, being careful not to twist, and pm to indicate beg of rnd (center back). Knit 5 rnds, then work 1 picot rnd (turning rnd) as foll:

PICOT RND: *K2tog, yo* rep to end of rnd.

Knit 5 rnds. Place provisionally cast-on sts on second needle. Next rnd, fold picot edge and knit CO sts together with live sts to form hem.

Rep Picot Rnd EOR twice. Knit even for 1".

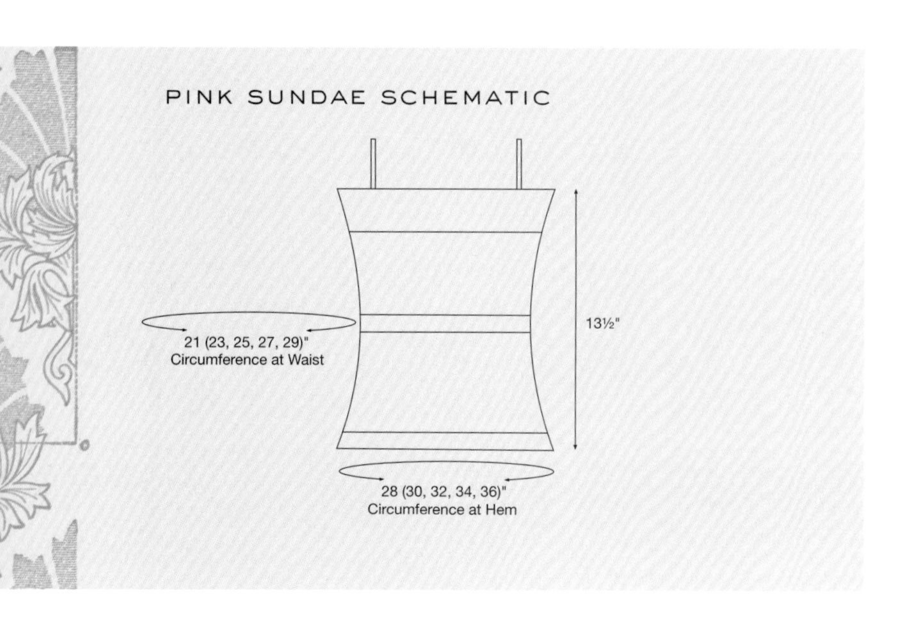

NEXT RND: K26 (28, 30, 32, 34) sts, pm, k47 (49, 51, 53, 55) sts, pm, k52 (56, 60, 64, 68) sts, pm, k47 (49, 51, 53, 55) sts, pm, k26 (28, 30, 32, 34) sts.

WAIST SHAPING

DEC RND: K26 (28, 30, 32, 34) sts, sm, k2tog, k to 2 sts before marker, ssk, bypass the "front" marker, k to next marker, sm, k2tog, k to 2 sts before next marker, ssk, k to end of rnd—194 (206, 218, 230, 242) sts rem. Knit even for 4 rnds.

Rep last 5 rnds 8 more times—162 (174, 186, 198, 210) sts rem.

Beg English Mesh Lace patt, working three 8-rnd repeats.

INC RND: Knit next rnd, increasing 18 sts evenly across rnd using M1 incs—180 (192, 204, 216, 228) sts. Cont in St st until work measures 3½" from end of English Mesh Lace.

Next rnd BO 2 sts, work to last 2 sts and BO 2 sts (total 4 sts bound off). Set work aside—176 (188, 200, 212, 224) sts rem.

WAVY BORDER

Using 2.75mm dpns and new ball of yarn, CO 21 sts. Work in Moss st for 5 rows.

Begin Wavy Border, working 14-row rep 20 (21, 22, 23, 24) times.

Work in Moss st for 2 rows.

NEXT (BUTTONHOLE) ROW: P1, k1, p2tog, yo, p1, k1, p1, p2tog, yo, k1, p1, k1, p2tog, yo, p1, k1, p1, p2tog, yo, k1, p1.

Work in Moss st for 2 rows. BO loosely in patt, do not break yarn.

FINISHING

Block pieces. Attach Wavy Border to body as foll:

With a new ball of yarn and 3mm circular needles, pick up 176 (188, 200, 212, 228) sts evenly along stockinette edge of Wavy Border between Moss st edges. Moss st edges will overlap at center back to form button and buttonhole bands, but will not be attached to body.

Lay body flat with RS of camisole back facing. Place border on top of body, right sides facing, so circular needle points are parallel.

Use yarn tail from Wavy Border to attach pieces using the three-needle bind-off (see Special Techniques, page 139).

Using dpns, make 2 I-cords, each approx 11" long for straps (see Special Techniques, page 139). Mark desired position on body, then sew on securely. Sew buttons opposite buttonholes. Weave in ends.

silken COWL TANK

zoë valette

Sleek, sexy, and silky! What more could a girl ask for from her hand-knits? Whether it's worn to work under a suit, paired with a long skirt for a holiday party, or worn with jeans to a trendy bar, the silken cowl does it all. This elegant little top skims your curves while the luscious silk yarn drapes softly against your skin. With just enough sparkle to make it stand out, the cowl neck will frame your face beautifully—no need for a necklace!

SIZES

XS (S, M, L, XL)

28–30 (32–34, 36–38, 40–42, 44–46)"

Shown in size XS

FINISHED MEASUREMENTS

CHEST: 30 (35, 38, 42, 46)"

BACK WAIST LENGTH: 21¾ (21¾, 22¼, 22¼, 22¾)"

COWL (DEPTH FROM CENTER FRONT): 10 (10, 10½, 10½, 11)"

YARN

YARN A: Tilli Tomas Pure and Simple (100% spun silk; 260 yards/100g): 2 (3, 3, 3, 4) skeins, American Beauty

YARN B: Tilli Tomas Disco Lights (100% spun silk with petite sequins; 225 yards/100g); 1 (1, 2, 2, 2) skeins, American Beauty

NEEDLES

4.5mm needles

4.5mm dpns or circulars, 16" long

NOTIONS

Stitch markers

Tapestry needle

GAUGE

31 sts and 45 rows = 4" in St st

pattern notes

This yarn is very inelastic. It is knit at a tighter gauge than recommended on the ball band to create a sturdier fabric. The ribbing, knit on the same size needles as the body, has virtually no recovery and does not draw in; this design feature allows the bottom edge and cowl to drape gracefully.

Zoë Valette has recently relocated to Michigan after spending several years in New Jersey. She teaches ballroom dancing and also manages to find time to knit, sew, crochet, and design. She loves to travel, and her favorite place to knit is in the car on a road trip—but not while driving!

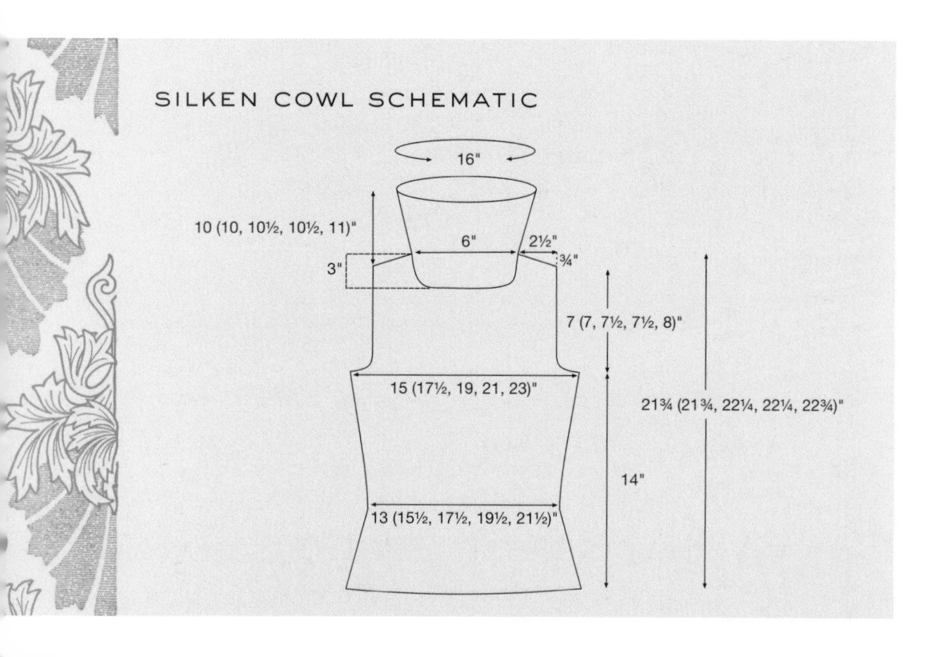
SILKEN COWL SCHEMATIC
16"
10 (10, 10½, 10½, 11)"
6"
2½"
¾"
3"
7 (7, 7½, 7½, 8)"
15 (17½, 19, 21, 23)"
21¾ (21¾, 22¼, 22¼, 22¾)"
14"
13 (15½, 17½, 19½, 21½)"

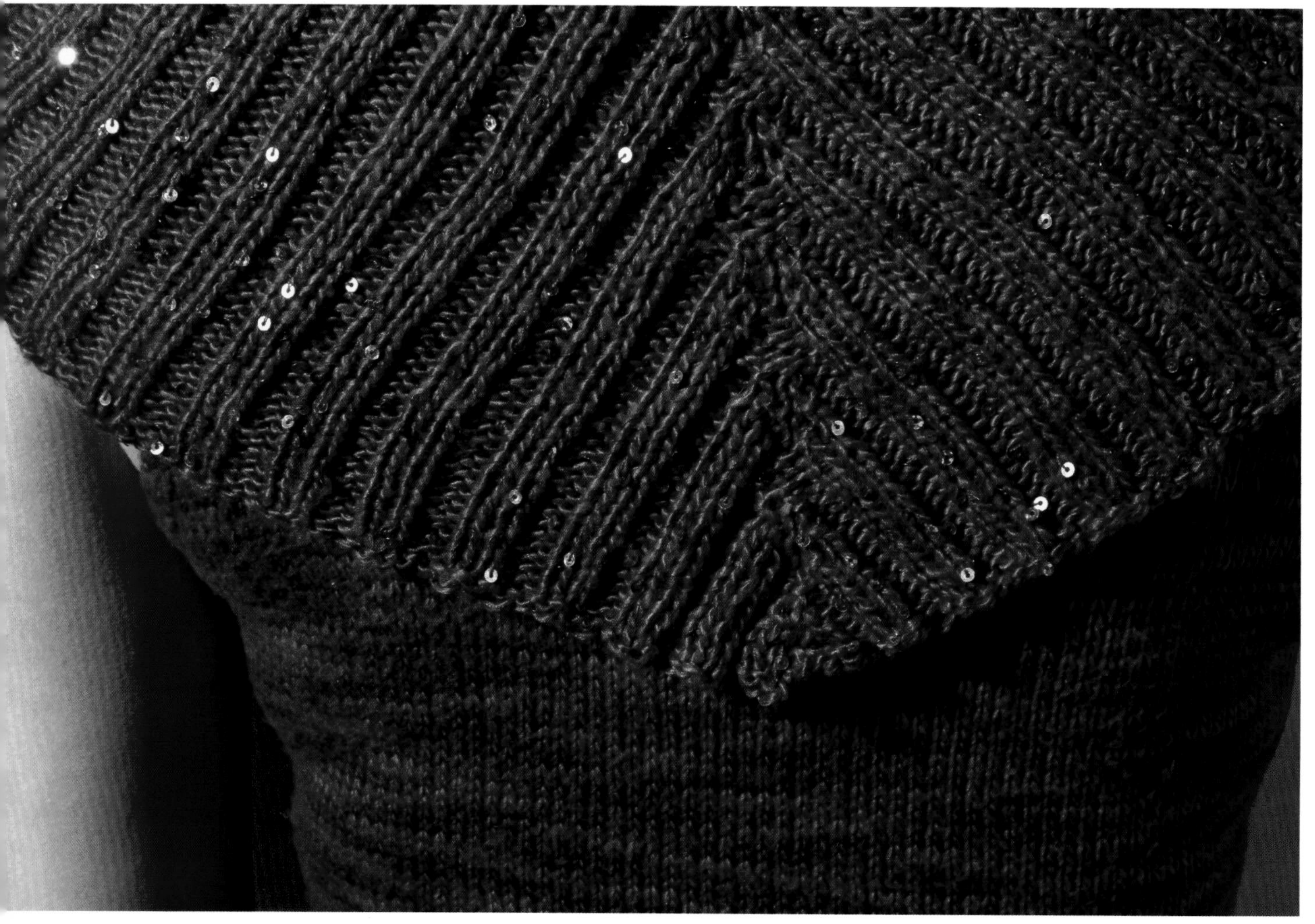

BACK

Using Yarn A, CO 86 (100, 110, 122, 134) st.

Work in k2, p2 rib for 6 rows, ending with WS row. Place markers 10 sts in from either edge to mark waist decs. Work even in St st until back measures 2½", ending with WS row.

WAIST SHAPING

DEC ROW: Knit across to first marker, sm, ssk, k across to 2 sts before marker, k2tog, sm, k to end. Work 5 more rows in St st.

Rep last 6 rows 4 more times—76 (90, 100, 112, 124) sts rem. Work even for 1".

INC ROW: Knit across to first marker, sm, m1, knit across to next marker, m1, pm, knit to end. Cont work 5 more rows in St st.

Rep last 6 rows 4 more times—86 (100, 110, 122, 134) sts rem. Work even until piece measures 14" from cast-on edge.

ARMHOLE SHAPING

BO 3 (4, 4, 5, 6) sts at beg of next 2 rows, then BO 2 (3, 4, 4, 5) sts at beg of next 2 rows. Pm 4 sts in from either edge to mark armhole decs. On all rem rows, slip the first st of each row to create a neat edge.

DEC ROW: Knit across to first marker, sm, ssk, knit across to 2 sts before marker, k2tog, sm, k to end.

Purl 1 row.

Rep last 2 rows 2 more times. Work Dec Row again, followed by 3 rows in St st. Rep last 4 rows two more times—64 (74, 82, 92, 100) sts rem. Work even until piece measures 6½ (6½, 7, 7, 7½)" from armhole BO, ending with WS row.

SHOULDER BIND-OFF

NECK BO: Knit 14 (17, 20, 23, 26) sts, join second ball of yarn, BO center 36 (40, 42, 46, 48) sts, knit to end. Work even for 1 row. At each armhole edge, BO 4 (5, 6, 7, 8) sts once, then BO 5 (6, 7, 8, 9) sts at twice.

FRONT

Work as for back until piece measures 4 (4, 4½, 4½, 5)" from armhole BO, ending with WS row.

Knit 22 (25, 28, 31, 34) sts, join second ball of yarn, BO center 20 (24, 26, 30, 32) sts, knit to end. Work even for 3 rows.

Begin neck shaping as foll: on first (left) shoulder, knit to last 4 sts, k2tog, k2; on second (right) shoulder, k2, ssk, knit across. Rep dec as set every RS row 7 more times—14 (17, 20, 23, 26) sts rem on each shoulder. Work even until piece measures 6½ (6½, 7, 7, 7½)" from armhole BO, ending with WS row. BO shoulders as for back.

Sew shoulder and side seams.

COWL

Using circular needle (or dpns, if preferred) and Yarn B, pick up sts around neck opening as foll:

With WS facing, pick up 36 (40, 42, 46, 48) sts along back neck, 4 sts on each back side of neck edge, 22 (25, 28, 31, 34) sts on each front side neck edge, and 22 (24, 26, 30, 32) sts along the center front—110 (124, 132, 146, 156) sts picked up. Place marker at center back. Work in k2, p2 rib in the rnd for 2 rnds.

On next and every other rnd, inc 1 st on either side of center back marker by knitting (or purling) into front and back of st on either side of marker. Maintain k2, p2 rib as set, working incs into patt.

Work until cowl measures 10 (10, 10½, 10½, 11)" from center front. Bind off loosely.

FINISHING

Weave in all ends and block.

betty v-neck VEST

andrea tung

This simply-styled vest is perfect worn over a crisp button-down shirt. Among its best features are the low V-neck, the shaped waist, saddle shoulders, and cable details along the arm.

SIZES

XS (S, M, L, XL)

32 (34, 36, 38, 40)"

Shown in size M

FINISHED MEASUREMENTS

unstretched

BUST: 32 (34, 36, 38, 40)"

LENGTH: 21 (21, 21, 23, 25)"

WAIST: 30 (32, 34, 36, 38)"

SHOULDERS: 14 (14½, 15, 15½, 16)"

YARN

Fable Handknit Pure Baby Alpaca (100% baby alpaca; 145 yards/50g): 8 (8, 8, 8, 10) skeins, Ethereal Blue (#01)

NEEDLES

4.0mm and 4.5mm straight needles

4.5mm circulars, 32" long

NOTIONS

Cable needle

Stitch holders

Tapestry needle

Crochet hook (optional)

GAUGE

19 sts and 24 rows = 4" in Rev St st on 4.5mm needles

pattern notes

The design is knit with two strands of yarn held together.

Read instructions completely before you begin, as short row shaping of shoulders occurs before completion of cable pattern; front neck shaping begins before waist shaping ends.

Andrea Tung is the founder of Fable Handknit (www.fablehandknit.com), a luxury yarn company. She has a degree in fashion design from Ryerson University and writes a fashion and knitting blog, Making Things (andreatung.blogspot.com).

STITCH PATTERN

REVERSE STOCKINETTE STITCH

ROW 1 (RS): Purl.

ROW 2: Knit.

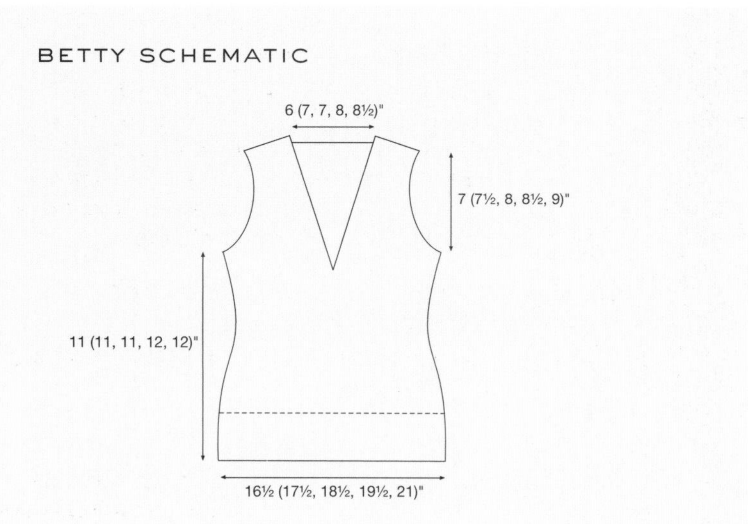

BACK

HEM

Using long-tail cast-on and 4mm needles, CO 80 (84, 90, 94, 100) sts with 2 strands of yarn held together. Work in k1, p1 rib for 4".

BODY

Change to larger needles and beg Rev St st.

DEC ROW (RS): P2tog, purl to end, p2tog.

Rep Dec Row every 6th row 3 (3, 3, 4, 4) times—72 (76, 82, 84, 90) sts rem. Work even for 18 rows.

INC ROW (WS): K1fb, work to end, k1fb. Work even for 5 rows.

Rep Inc Row once. Work even for 7 rows.

Rep Inc Row one more time—78 (82, 88, 92, 98) sts.

Work even until piece measures 11 (11, 11, 12, 12)" from cast-on edge, end with WS row.

ARMHOLE SHAPING

On RS, BO 5 sts at beg of next 2 rows. Work Dec Row EOR 2 times—64 (68, 74, 78, 84) sts. Work even for 1 (3, 1, 3, 1) rows.

CABLES

On WS, beg cable patt:

ROW 1 AND ALL WS ROWS: K4, p8, k4, knit to last 12 sts, p8, k4.

ROW 2 AND ALL RS ROWS: P4, k8, purl to last 12 sts, k8, p4.

On Row 12 (12, 14, 14, 16): P4, sl 4 sts onto cn to front of work, k4, knit sts on cn, purl to last 12 sts, sl 4 sts onto cn to back of work, k4, p4. Rep through Row 12 (12, 14, 14, 16) 2 more times.

SHOULDER SHAPING

Rep Rows 1 and 2 of cable patt one more time,

And AT THE SAME TIME, beg working short rows (see Special Techniques, page 138, for additional information).

ROWS 1–2: Work to last 4 sts on next 2 rows, wrap, turn.

ROWS 3–4: Work to last 13 sts on next 2 rows, wrap, turn work.

ROWS 5–6: Work rows picking up wraps.

Work 18 (18, 20, 22, 24) sts, BO center 28 (34, 34, 38, 40) sts, work to end. Place rem sts on holders—18 (18, 20, 22, 24) sts each side.

FRONT

HEM

Using long-tail method and smaller needles, CO 80 (84, 90, 94, 100) sts with 2 strands of yarn held together. Work in k1, p1 rib for 4".

BODY

Change to larger needles and beg Rev St st.

DEC ROW (RS): P2tog, purl to end, p2tog.

Rep Dec Row every 6th row 3 (3, 3, 4, 4) times. Work even for 18 rows.

NECK SHAPING

Continue Inc Rows as for back, and AT THE SAME TIME, beg neck shaping as foll:

On Row 44 (44, 48, 54, 54), work to the center; attach new ball of yarn and work to end of row. Working both sides at same time, dec 1 st at each neck edge EOR, 2 times, then every 4th row, 13 times as foll: at left neck edge work dec as p2tog; at right neck edge work dec as p2tog tbl.

ARMHOLE AND SHOULDER SHAPING

Complete armholes, cables, and shoulder shaping as for back.

FINISHING

Block pieces to measurements. Finish shoulders using three-needle bind-off (see Special Techniques, page 137). Sew side seams. Weave in ends.

NECK RIB

With circular needle, evenly pick up sts along both sides of front and back neck. Do not join for working in the rnd. Work in k1, p1 rib for 6 rows. BO in rib. Fold outer corners of front center to inside and join at center.

ARMHOLE TRIM

Using circular needle and crochet hook, if desired, evenly pick up sts along armholes beg at underarm seam. BO.

lace panel TWIN SET

connie chang chinchio

This delicate camisole can be worn alone or paired with its coordinating cardigan. Either way, with its pretty lace side panels—worked in an open diamond lattice—it'll make you feel as special as the rare, premium-grade alpaca it's worked in. The clean, luxuriously soft alpaca perfectly complements the spare, three-quarter-sleeve cardigan with a yoke worked in lace. A round scoop neck and small, elegant cream buttons complete the picture.

SIZES

XXS (XS, S, M, L, XL, 2X)

32 (34, 36, 38, 40, 42, 44)"

Shown in size XXS

FINISHED MEASUREMENTS

unstretched

CHEST: 32 (34, 36, 38, 40, 42, 44)"

LENGTH (CAMISOLE): 17¾ (17¾, 18¼, 18½, 19, 19¼, 19¾)"

LENGTH (CARDIGAN): 18½ (18½, 19, 19¼, 19¾, 20, 20½)"

YARN

CAMISOLE: Blue Sky Alpacas Royal Alpaca (100% alpaca; 288 yards/100g): 2 (2, 2, 3, 3, 3, 3) skeins, Petticoat (706)

CARDIGAN: Blue Sky Alpacas Royal Alpaca (100% alpaca; 288 yards/100g): 3 (4, 4, 4, 5, 5, 6) skeins, Petticoat (706)

NEEDLES

2.75mm circulars, 32" long

3.25mm circulars, 32" long

NOTIONS

Tapestry needle

Stitch markers

Stitch holders

Seven small buttons for cardigan

GAUGE

28 sts and 38 rows = 4" in St st

pattern notes

The lace panels are slightly stretchy. The camisole is knit slightly smaller than measured chest size to accommodate for this. To maintain the integrity of the lace panels, all increases are worked in the Stockinette stitch portion of the camisole.

Knit in the round up to the armholes, the front and back of the camisole are then worked flat. When working in the round, alternate (even-numbered) rows in the lace chart are knit. When worked flat, alternate rows are purled.

When decreasing for the cardigan neck, maintain lace pattern. When too few stitches are available to complete an entire chart repeat, be sure every decrease (ssk, k2tog) is paired with an increase (yo); and every double decrease (sl 1, k2tog, psso) is paired with two increases.

Read instructions carefully before beginning; yoke, armhole, and waist shapings are worked at the same time. Short row shaping may be used for shoulders, allowing for neater three-needle bind-off (see Special Techniques, page 139).

Connie first started kitting obsessively six years ago in graduate school while studying physics, but has only recently started designing. Her designs are featured in Knitter's *and* Magknits.com. *When her husband can tear her away from her yarn habit, Connie also enjoys hiking, traveling, and cooking. She blogs about her life—knitting and otherwise—at physicsknits.blogspot.com.*

STITCH PATTERNS

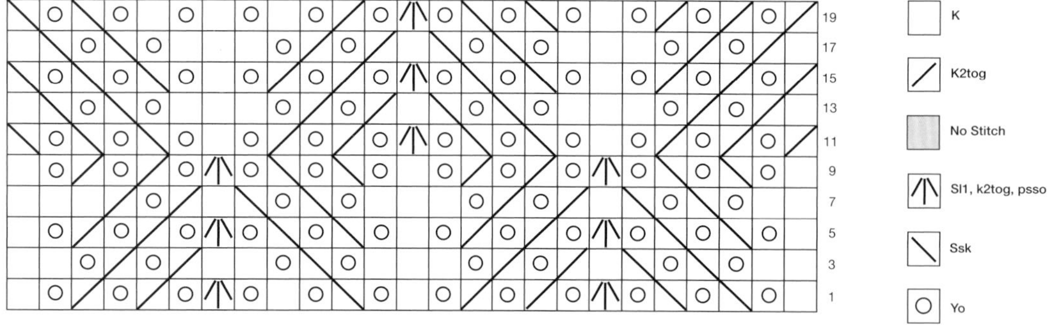

Lace Panel Camisole Chart

- K
- K2tog
- No Stitch
- Sl1, k2tog, psso
- Ssk
- Yo

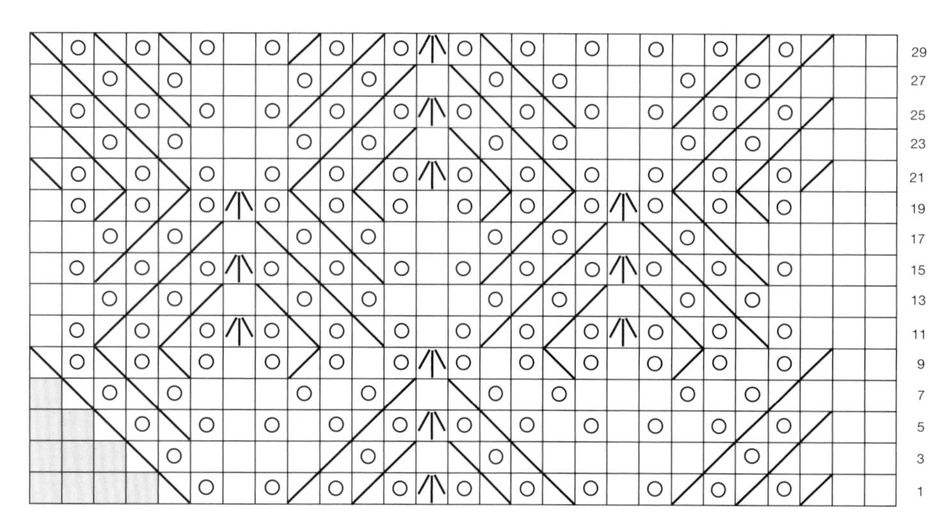

Lace Panel Cardigan Chart: Sizes 32" and 34"- Right Front, Reverse for Left Front

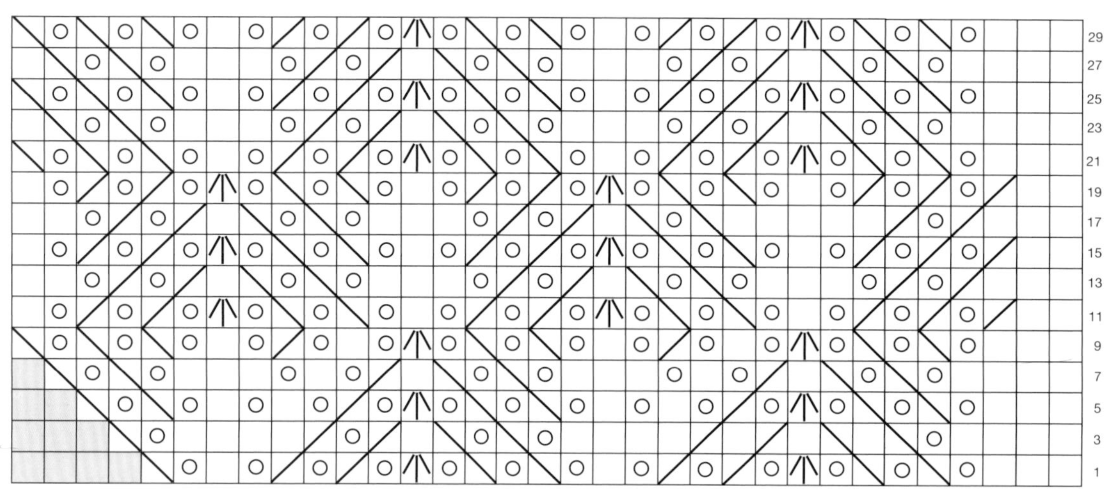

Lace Panel Cardigan Chart: Sizes 36", 38", 40", 42", 44" - Right Front, Reverse for Left Front

SEED STITCH

(multiple of 2 sts, 2-row repeat)

ROW 1: *K1, p1; rep from * to end.

ROW 2: *P1, k1; rep from * to end.

Rep Rows 1 and 2.

CAMISOLE

BODY

Using 3.25mm needles, CO 186 (200, 214, 228, 242, 256, 270) st. Join for working in the rnd, being careful not to twist sts, and pm to indicate beg of rnd.

Work set-up rnd: Work Row 1 of 25-st lace chart, pm, k68 (75, 82, 89, 96, 103, 110) sts, pm, work Row 1 of lace chart, pm, k68 (75, 82, 89, 96, 103, 110) sts. Work even foll chart as set for 16 rows.

BUST SHAPING

Beg Row 17 of lace chart, and AT THE SAME TIME beg Inc Rnd: Work to 2nd marker, k2, M1R, work to 2 sts before 3rd marker, M1L, k2, work to 4th marker, k2, M1R, work to 2 sts before end of rnd, M1L, k2.

Work 13 rnds as established.

Rep Inc Rnd every 14th rnd 5 more times—210 (224, 238, 252, 266, 280, 294) sts rem.

Work even until body measures 10¾ (10¾, 10¾, 11, 11, 11¼, 11¼)" from bottom of cast-on edge.

DIVIDE FOR FRONT AND BACK

BACK

The sts of each lace panel will be divided evenly between the back and front. Maintain lace patt at sides and cont St st between panels as foll:

Work 13 sts, BO 4 sts, work to 3rd marker, work first 12 sts of lace chart, placing rem sts on holder or spare needle for front, turn.

Next row BO 4 sts, work to end.

Rep last row until a total of 24 sts have been bound off—80 (87, 94, 101, 108, 115, 122) sts rem.

At each armhole edge, dec 2 sts EOR 0 (1, 2, 4, 4, 6, 6) times, then 1 st EOR 8 (8, 8, 6, 7, 5, 7) times.

BO rem 64 (67, 70, 73, 78, 81, 84) sts.

FRONT

With RS facing, attach yarn to armhole edge and shape as foll:

At each armhole edge, BO 5 sts once, then BO 4 sts twice—80 (87, 94, 101, 108, 115, 122) sts rem.

XXS ONLY

NEXT ROW: K1, ssk, k35, BO 4 sts, k35, k2tog, k1.

XS (S, M) ONLY

NEXT ROW: K1, ssk, ssk, k36 (39, 42), BO 5 (6, 7) sts, k36 (39, 42), k2tog, k2tog, k1.

L (XL, XXL) ONLY

NEXT ROW (RS): K1, ssk, ssk, k98 (105, 112), k2tog, k2tog, k1.

NEXT ROW (WS): Work even.

NEXT ROW (RS): K1, ssk, ssk, k43 (45, 48), BO 8 (11, 12) sts, k43 (45, 48), k2tog, k2tog, k1.

RIGHT FRONT

Continue armhole shaping as for back (working even once all armhole dec are made) and AT THE SAME TIME work neck shaping as foll:

BO 4 sts at neck edge every RS row 2 (2, 2, 2, 3, 3, 3) times.

BO 3 sts at neck edge every RS row 6 (6, 6, 7, 6, 6, 6) times.

Dec 1 st at neck edge every RS row 2 (3, 4, 2, 3, 3, 4) times.

BO rem 2 sts.

LEFT FRONT

Attach yarn to neck edge, and work as for the right front, reversing neck and shoulder shaping.

FINISHING

Adjust number of sts picked up as necessary for a smooth finish. Use smaller needles for all borders.

ARMHOLE BORDERS

With RS facing and smaller circular needle, pick up 54 (58, 62, 64, 67, 69, 74) sts around the armhole—starting from the top of the triangular right front tip and ending at the beg of BO edge of back. Work in Seed st until border is ½" wide, ending with WS row. BO all sts in St st.

BACK BORDER

With RS facing and smaller circular needle, pick up 72 (75, 78, 81, 86, 89, 92) sts across the BO sts from the right armhole border, the back, and the left armhole border. Work in Seed st until border is ½" wide, ending with WS row. BO all sts in St st.

FRONT BORDER

With RS facing and smaller circular needle, pick up 63 (65, 68, 70, 75, 77, 80) sts across front. Work in Seed st until border measures ½", ending with WS row. BO all sts in St st.

LEFT STRAP

With RS facing and smaller circular needle, pick up 9 sts from the top triangular point of the left front across BO sts of armhole border and front border. Working in Seed st, dec 1 st on both ends EOR until 3 sts rem. These 3 sts will form I-cord strap.

Work I-cord to desired length and attach to back piece.

Rep for right strap.

Weave in all ends and block.

CARDIGAN

BACK

Using 3.25mm needles, CO 102 (108, 116, 122, 130, 136, 144) sts.

Work 6 rows in Seed st.

Work 10 rows in St st.

WAIST SHAPING

INC RND: K2, M1R, work in St st to 2 sts before end, M1L, k2.

Rep inc rnd every 14th row 5 times more—114 (120, 128, 134, 142, 148, 156) sts.

Work even in St st until body measures 11 (11, 11, 11¼, 11¼, 11½, 11½)" from cast-on edge, ending with a WS row.

ARMHOLE SHAPING

BO 4 (5, 6, 6, 7, 7, 8) sts at the beg of next two rows.

Work even for 1 row.

NEXT ROW (RS): K2, ssk, k to last 4 sts, k2tog, k2.

NEXT ROW (WS): Work even.

Rep last two rows 4 (4, 5, 6, 6, 7, 8) times more—96 (100, 104, 108, 114, 118, 122) sts rem.

Work even until armhole measures 6½ (6½, 7, 7, 7½, 7½, 8)", ending with WS row.

BACK NECK SHAPING

NEXT ROW (RS): K25 (27, 27, 29, 29, 31, 33), place center 46 (46, 50, 50, 56, 56, 56) sts on holder, attach yarn to next st, k25 (27, 27, 29, 29, 31, 33).

Working both sides at same time with separate balls of yarn, work even for 1 row.

At each neck edge, dec 1 st this row, then EOR 1 time.

SHOULDER SHAPING

Beg RS row, BO rem sts over next 5 rows as foll: At armhole edge, BO 7 (8, 8, 9, 9, 9, 10) sts once, 8 (8, 8, 9, 9, 10, 10) sts once, then BO rem 8 (9, 9, 9, 9, 10, 11) sts.

LEFT FRONT

Using 3.25mm needles, CO 51 (54, 58, 61, 65, 68, 72) sts.

Work 6 rows in Seed st.

Work 10 rows in St st.

WAIST SHAPING

INC RND: K2, M1R, k to end.

Rep Inc Rnd every 14th row 5 times more—57 (60, 64, 67, 71, 74, 78) sts.

Work even until piece measures 10 (10, 10, 10¼, 10¼, 10½, 10½)" from cast-on edge, ending with RS row.

LACE YOKE

SET-UP ROW (WS): Dec 2 sts evenly over first 27 (27, 33, 33, 33, 33, 33) sts to account for slight difference in gauge between St st and lace patt st—55 (58, 62, 65, 69, 72, 76) sts rem.

ROW 1 (RS): K32 (35, 33, 36, 40, 43, 47), beg Row 1 of lace chart for the appropriate size over rem 23 (23, 29, 29, 29, 29, 29) sts.

ROW 2 AND ALL WS ROWS: Purl.

ROW 3 (RS): K31 (34, 32, 35, 39, 42, 46), work Row 3 of lace chart over next 24 (24, 30, 30, 30, 30, 30) sts.

Cont in this manner, increasing the lace panel by 1 st and decreasing the St st portion by 1 st until lace panel contains 27 (27, 33, 33, 33, 33, 33) sts.

Work as estab with the first 28 (31, 29, 32, 36, 39, 43) sts in St st, foll by 27 (27, 33, 33, 33, 33, 33) sts of lace panel. Complete Rows 1–30 of lace chart one time, then Rows 11–30 to end.

ARMHOLE SHAPING

AT THE SAME TIME, when piece measures 11 (11, 11, 11¼, 11¼, 11½, 11½)" from cast-on edge, ending with WS row, beg armhole shaping as follows:

At beg of next (RS) row BO 4 (5, 6, 6, 7, 7, 8) sts once, then dec EOR 5 (5, 6, 7, 7, 8, 9) times—46 (48, 50, 52, 55, 57, 59) sts rem.

AT THE SAME TIME, when armhole measures 2", beg neck decs on WS as foll:

NECK SHAPING

At neck edge, BO 8 (8, 9, 9, 10, 10, 10) sts once, then BO 2 sts EOR 3 (3, 3, 3, 4, 4, 4) times.

Dec 1 st EOR 4 times (all sizes), then dec 1 st every 4th row 5 (5, 6, 6, 6, 6, 6) times—23 (25, 25, 27, 27, 29, 31) total sts rem, including 4 (4, 8, 8, 5, 5, 5) sts in lace st.

Work even until armhole measures 7 (7, 7½, 7½, 8, 8, 8½)", ending with WS row.

SHOULDER SHAPING

Beg at armhole edge (RS), BO shoulder sts over next 5 rows as for back shoulder.

RIGHT FRONT

Work as for left front, reversing all shaping. Lace chart is reversed for all sizes. Lace panel chart will be worked first, followed by St st.

SLEEVES (MAKE 2)

Using 3.25mm needles, CO 64 (68, 70, 74, 78, 82, 88) sts.

Work 2 rows in St st.

INC RND: K1, M1R, k to last st, M1L, k1.

Rep Inc Rnd every 10th row 8 (8, 9, 9, 9, 9, 8) times more—82 (86, 90, 94, 98, 102, 106) sts.

Work even until sleeve measures 9½ (9½, 10, 10, 10¼, 10¼, 10½)", ending with WS row.

SLEEVE CAP SHAPING

BO 4 (5, 6, 6, 7, 7, 8) sts at beg of next 2 rows—74 (76, 78, 82, 84, 88, 90) sts rem.

Dec 1 st each end of sleeve every row 6 (6, 6, 6, 6, 8, 8) times EOR 4 (4, 4, 4, 5, 4, 5) times, then every 4th row 4 (4, 4, 4, 4, 4, 4) times—46 (48, 50, 54, 54, 56, 56) sts rem.

Dec 1 st each end of sleeve EOR 4 (4, 5, 5, 6, 6, 7) times then EOR 4 (4, 5, 5, 5, 5, 5) times—30 (32, 30, 34, 32, 34, 32) sts rem.

BO 3 (3, 3, 4, 3, 4, 3) sts at beg of next 2 rows, then 3 (4, 3, 4, 4, 4, 4) sts at beg of next 2 rows.

BO rem 18 sts.

FINISHING

Block pieces to measurements. Sew shoulder seams together. Set sleeves into armholes, easing in any fullness at top of sleeve. Sew sleeve and side seams.

Adjust number of picked up stitches if necessary.

BUTTON BAND

With RS facing and smaller circular needle, pick up 92 (92, 92, 93, 93, 95, 95) sts from left front edge. Work in Seed st until band measures ½", ending with WS row. BO in St st.

BUTTONHOLE BAND

With RS facing and smaller circular needle, pick up 92 (92, 92, 93, 93, 95, 95) sts from right front edge. Work in Seed st until band measures ½" ending with WS row.

NEXT ROW: Maintaining Seed st patt, work 8 (8, 8, 9, 9, 7, 5) sts, work 3-st buttonhole, *work 10 (10, 10, 10, 10, 11, 11) sts, work 3-st buttonhole, rep from * 5 times more, work 3 sts.

Continue in Seed st until band width measures ½", ending with WS row.

BO in St st.

NECK BAND

With RS facing and smaller circular needle, pick up 56 (56, 61, 61, 67, 67, 71) sts from the right front neck edge, 55 (55, 59, 59, 65, 65, 65) sts from back neck edge, and 56 (56, 61, 61, 67, 67, 71) sts from the left front neck edge—167 (167, 181, 181, 199, 199, 207) total sts picked up.

Work in Seed st for ½" ending with WS row. BO in St st.

SLEEVE BANDS

With RS facing and smaller circular needle and starting at underarm seam, pick up 64 (68, 70, 74, 78, 82, 88). Do not join in the rnd to leave a side slit at the band. Work in Seed st for ½", ending with WS row. BO in St st.

Sew buttons opposite buttonholes.

Weave in ends. Block again if desired.

TWIN SET SCHEMATICS

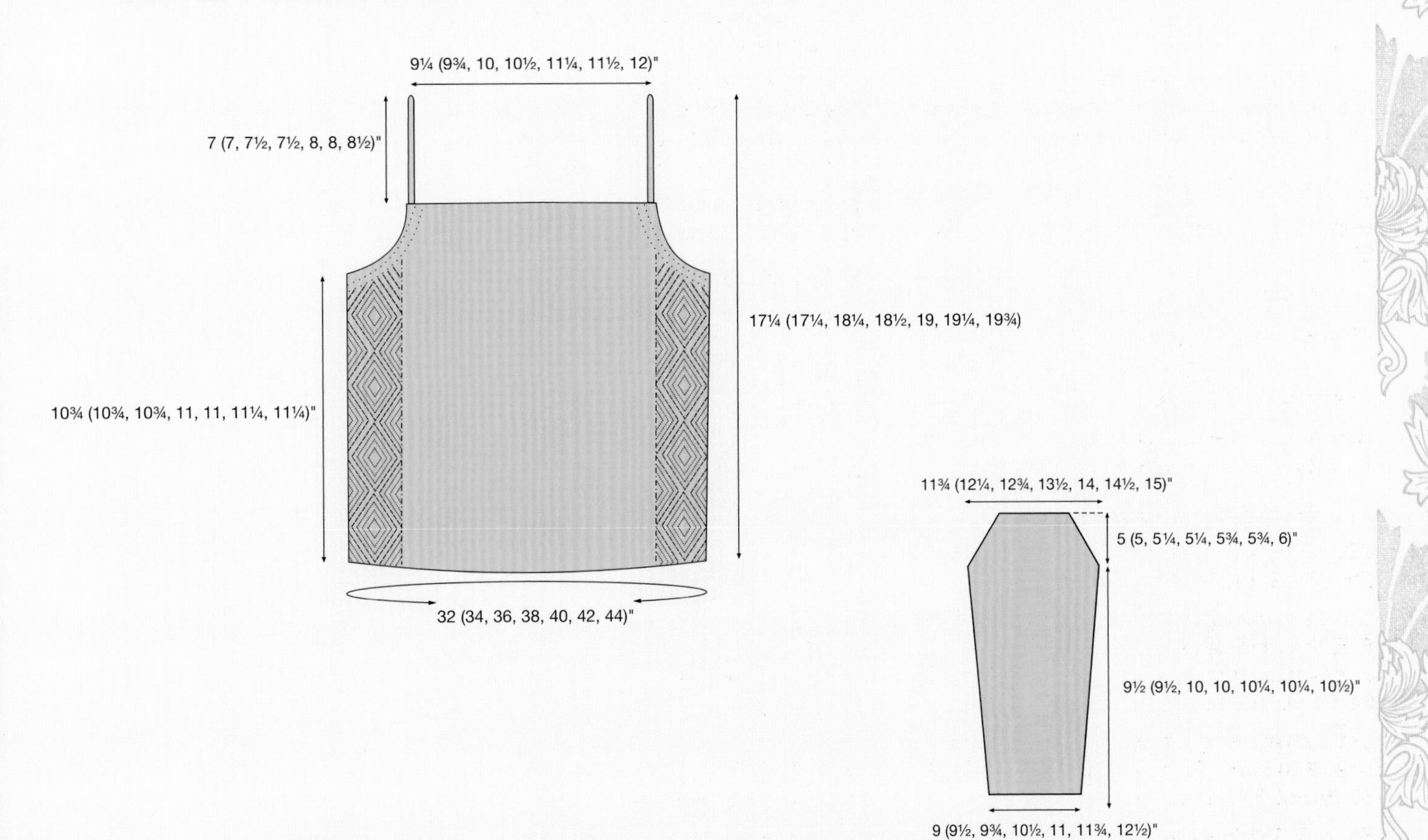

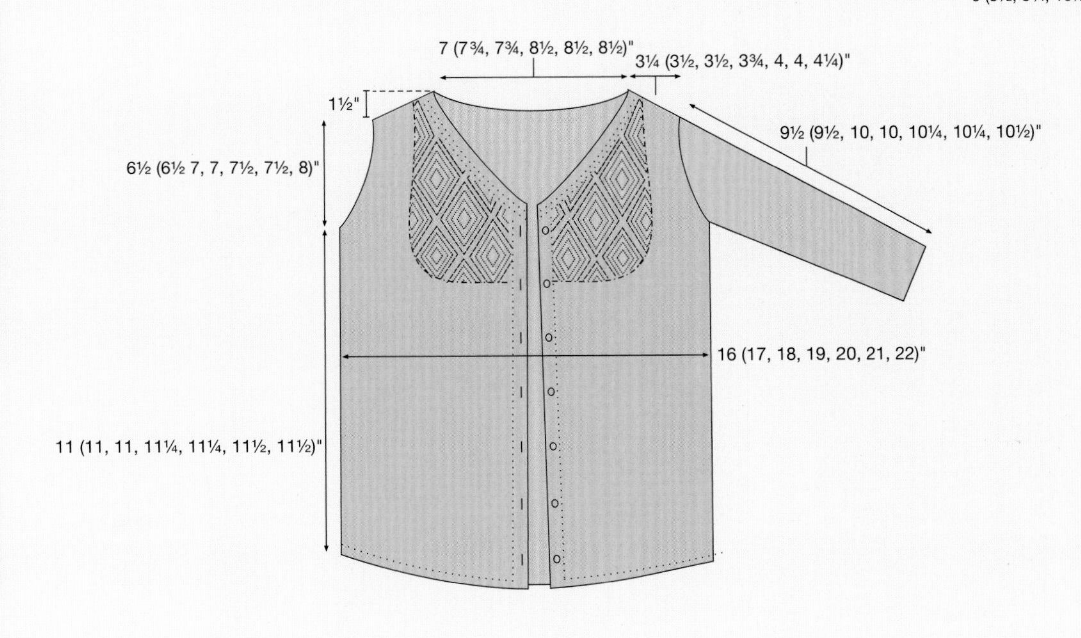

CHAPTER TWO

SENSUAL CHIC

modern sweaters with hip details

mcqueen SWEATER

yahaira ferreira

With its modern fit; deep, plunging cowl; and heavenly cashmere, this sweater, inspired by an Alexander McQueen runway knit, is the sexy girl's uniform. Wear it with a pencil skirt to go from day to night, cinch it with a belt for a dress, or wear it backwards for an even more risqué look. The bishop sleeves add a bit of whimsy and contrast as another nod to McQueen.

SIZES

XXS (XS, S, M, L, XL, 2X)

32 (34, 36, 38, 40, 42, 44)"

Shown in size XL

FINISHED MEASUREMENTS

unstretched

CHEST: 31 (33, 35, 37, 39, 41, 43)"

LENGTH: 26¾ (27, 29, 29, 29, 29, 29½)"

YARN

Laines du Nord Royal Cashmere (100% Italian cashmere; 82 yards/25g): 16 (17, 18, 19, 20, 21, 23) skeins, Sky (19)

NEEDLES

5mm and 5.5mm circulars, 32" long

NOTIONS

Stitch markers

Stitch holder

Tapestry needle

GAUGE

16 sts and 26 rows = 4" in St st with 5.5mm needles

pattern notes

Read instructions carefully before beginning; back neck is shaped at the same time as waist is increased. Rows are worked flat beginning at left back neck. Both shapings may occur in the same row. For a deeper or shallower back neckline, begin shaping earlier or later.

This pattern uses full-fashion shaping; increases and decreases are always done two stitches in from either edge, even when not stated.

BODY

HEM

Using tubular cast-on (see Special Techniques, page 139) and 5.5mm circular needle, CO 132 (138, 146, 154, 158, 166, 172) sts. Pm and join for working in the rnd, taking care not to twist sts. Work in k1, p1 rib for 3", placing marker for side seam after 66 (69, 73, 77, 79, 83, 86) sts.

NEXT RND: Inc 2 (2, 2, 2, 2, 2, 4) sts evenly across the rnd to 134 (140, 148, 156, 160, 168, 176) sts total.

Switch to St st and work for 1 (1, 1, 1, 1½, 1½, 1½)".

WAIST SHAPING

DEC RND: *K2, ssk, work to 4 sts before marker, k2tog, k2, sm; rep from * one time (4 sts dec).

Rep Dec Rnd every 5th (7th, 6th, 6th, 7th, 7th) rnd 7 (6, 7, 7, 6, 6, 6) times—102 (112, 116, 124, 132, 140, 148) sts rem.

Work even for 1".

BACK SHAPING SET-UP ROW: Work to side seam marker, sm, work 14 (15, 16, 17, 18, 19, 20) sts of back, BO next 23 (26, 26, 28, 30, 32, 34) sts. Rows now begin at this point (left back shoulder) and will be worked flat.

Work rem 14 (15, 16, 17, 18, 19, 20) sts.

The foll rows include both back neck decs and waistline shaping (incs). Pay careful attention to the simultaneous shaping

Beg at left back neck edge (after BO sts), k2, ssk, work to 2 sts before left side marker, M1L, k2, sm, k2, M1R, work to 2 sts before right side marker, M1L, k2, sm, k2, M1R, work to last 4 sts, k2tog, k2—2 sts dec at back neck; 4 sts inc at waist.

Rep inc shaping every foll 10th (10th, 8th, 8th, 8th, 8th 8th) row 4 (4, 5, 5, 5, 5, 5) times, and AT THE SAME TIME, complete neck decs as set EOR 3 (2, 3, 2, 4, 2, 3) times—91 (100, 106, 114, 116, 126, 130) sts rem.

Work even until piece measures 15¾ (16¼, 16½, 16¾, 16¾, 17, 17¼)" from cast-on edge.

DIVIDE FOR ARMHOLE

(RS) Knit all sts for left back and front, stopping at side marker. Transfer 61 (66, 70, 74, 78, 82, 86) sts just knit to holder for front. Working on right back section only, with RS facing to start, beg armhole shaping.

RIGHT ARMHOLE

BO 2 (3, 3, 3, 3, 4, 4) sts at beg of next row.

Work one row even

DEC ROW: K2, ssk, work to end

Rep Dec Row EOR 2 (2, 3, 4, 5, 5, 6) times more—10 (11, 11, 12, 10, 12, 11) sts rem.

LEFT ARMHOLE

Attach second ball of yarn at left back neck edge and work one (RS) row.

BO 2 (3, 3, 3, 3, 4, 4) sts at beg next (WS) row.

DEC ROW: P2, p2tog, work to end.

Rep Dec Row EOR 2 (2, 3, 4, 5, 5, 6) times more—10 (11, 11, 12, 10, 12, 11) sts rem.

Work even until armhole measures 7¾ (7¾, 8, 8, 8¼, 8½, 8½)".

SHOULDER SHAPING

SIZE XXS (XS, S, XXL)

Place sts on holder.

SIZE M (L, XL)

For left back shoulder, knit to last 5 (5, 6) sts at armhole edge, wrap and turn (see Special Techniques, page 138).

Purl one row.

Knit to 6 (6, 7) sts at armhole edge, w/t.

Purl one row.

Knit one row, picking up wraps.

Place rem sts on holder.

For right back shoulder, complete as for first shoulder.

FRONT

Transfer front sts from holder to needle. With RS facing, join yarn. Shape front armholes as for back. Continue until armhole measures 5 (5, 5¼, 5, 5, 5½, 5¼, 5¾)"—51 (54, 56, 58, 60, 62, 64) sts rem.

NECK SHAPING

Work 15 (16, 17, 18, 18, 19, 19) sts, slip next 21 (22, 22, 22, 24, 24, 26) sts to holder, and with second ball of yarn, work rem 15 (16, 17, 18, 18, 19, 19) sts. Dec 1 st at neck edge every row 6 (6, 7, 7, 7, 6, 7) times—9 (10, 10, 11, 11, 13, 12) sts rem.

Work even until armhole measures 7¾ (7¾, 8, 8, 8¼, 8½, 8½)". Complete front shoulder shaping as for back. Join front and back shoulder seams with Three-needle bind-off (see Special Techniques, page 139).

MCQUEEN SCHEMATICS

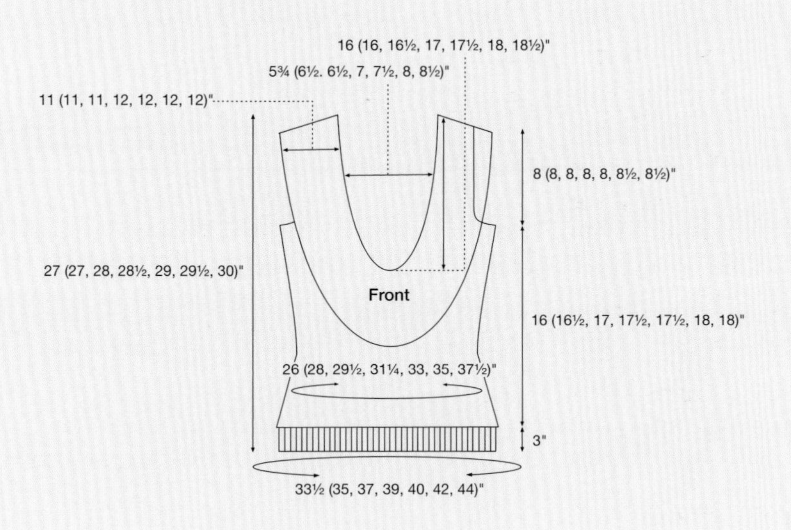

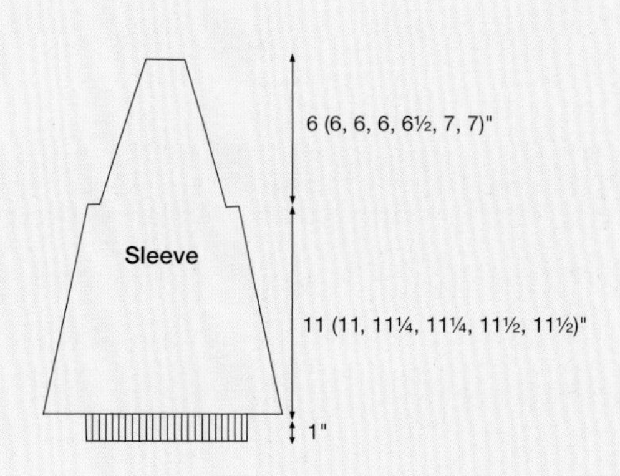

SLEEVES (MAKE 2)

HEM

Using tubular cast-on (see Special Techniques, page 139) and 5mm needles, CO 39 (40, 41, 43, 45, 48, 51) sts. Join for working in the rnd; pm. Work in k1, p1 rib for 1".

Change to 5.5mm needles and St st. Inc 39 (40, 41, 43, 45, 48, 51) sts evenly across rnd—78 (80, 82, 86, 90, 96, 102) sts total. Work 1" even.

DEC RND: K1, ssk, knit to last 3 sts, k2tog, k1—76 (78, 80, 84, 88, 94, 100) sts rem.

Rep Dec Rnd every 3rd rnd 8 (11, 10, 14, 16, 14, 15) times, then

Every 4th rnd 7 (4, 6, 3, 3, 4, 3) times, and

Every 2nd row 0 (1, 1, 2, 0, 2, 2) times—46 (46, 49, 51, 50, 54, 60) sts rem.

Work even until sleeve measures 11 (11, 11¼, 11¼, 11½, 11½, 11½)" excluding hem.

CAP SHAPING

BO 2 (3, 3, 3, 3, 4, 4) sts at beg next 2 rows—42 (40, 43, 45, 46, 46, 48) sts rem.

Dec 1 st each end every 2nd (2nd, 2nd, 2nd, 2nd, 3rd, 2nd) row 3 (2, 2, 4, 3, 7, 3) times, then every 3rd (3rd, 3rd, 3rd, 3rd, 4th) row 8 (10, 10, 8, 10, 10, 10) times.

Dec 1 st each end of every 2nd (2nd, 2nd, 2nd, 2nd, 2nd, 3rd) row 3 (1, 2, 3, 2, 7, 3) time(s).

BO rem 14 (14, 15, 15, 16, 16, 16) sts loosely.

FINISHING

Block pieces to size. Set in sleeves. Weave in ends.

COWL

Cowl is worked in the rnd.

With WS of work facing and 5mm needles, pick up and knit 3 out of every 4 sts from left back neck edge, right back neck edge, right front neck edge, 21 (22, 22, 22, 24, 24) sts from front neck holder, and 3 out of 4 from left front neck edge.

Pm and join for working in rnd. Work even in k1, p1 rib until collar measures 11 (11, 11, 12, 12, 12, 12)" or desired length. BO loosely as foll:

Work 2 sts in patt (either knit or purl). Wyib *transfer the 2 worked sts to the LH needle, and k2togtbl. Work 1 st in patt (move yarn to back if it was a purl), rep from *.

sayuri SWEATER

joelene wiggins

SIZES

XS (S, M, L, XL)

32–34 (36–38, 40–42, 44–46, 48–50)"

Shown in size XS

FINISHED MEASUREMENTS

unstretched

BUST: 35¼ (39¼, 44, 48, 52)"

LENGTH: 26 (27, 29¼, 30¼, 32)"

WAIST CIRCUMFERENCE: 31¼ (33½, 36¼, 40, 43¾)"

YARN

Louisa Harding Grace Silk & Wool (50% Merino Wool, 50% Silk; 110 yards/50g): 11 (13, 14, 15, 17) skeins, Teal (7)

NEEDLES

5mm circular needles, 32" long

4.5mm dpns

NOTIONS

Stitch markers

Sewing needle

GAUGE

20 sts and 24 rows = 4" in St st

Sayuri was designed to have a modern look with a kimono feel. The texture of the Linen stitch adds even more depth and draws in the waist, creating an hourglass shape for any body type. The wool/silk blend of the yarn offers just enough sheen and drape, making it the perfect sweater for an evening out. Though dressy, there is nothing fussy about the design—it's the perfect sweater to throw on with jeans and heels. Wearers convey a sense of easy-going luxury.

pattern notes

When picking a size, note that sweater is meant to be loose in the bust and fitted in the waist.

This sweater has a slightly unusual construction. The upper back is knit flat from waist to shoulders. After neck bind-off, fronts are worked separately down to waist and joined to form a "V." Provisional cast-on is then removed, fronts and back joined, and remainder of sweater is knit in the round to the hem.

Joelene is one crafty gal. When she's not spending her days enjoying the beautiful California weather with her husband, Daniel, and dog, Vito, she's obsessing about sock yarn or on a quest to find the perfect 2.25mm needles. Besides knitting and crocheting, Joelene is the mastermind behind misocrafty knitting bags. Visit her site www.misocrafty.com.

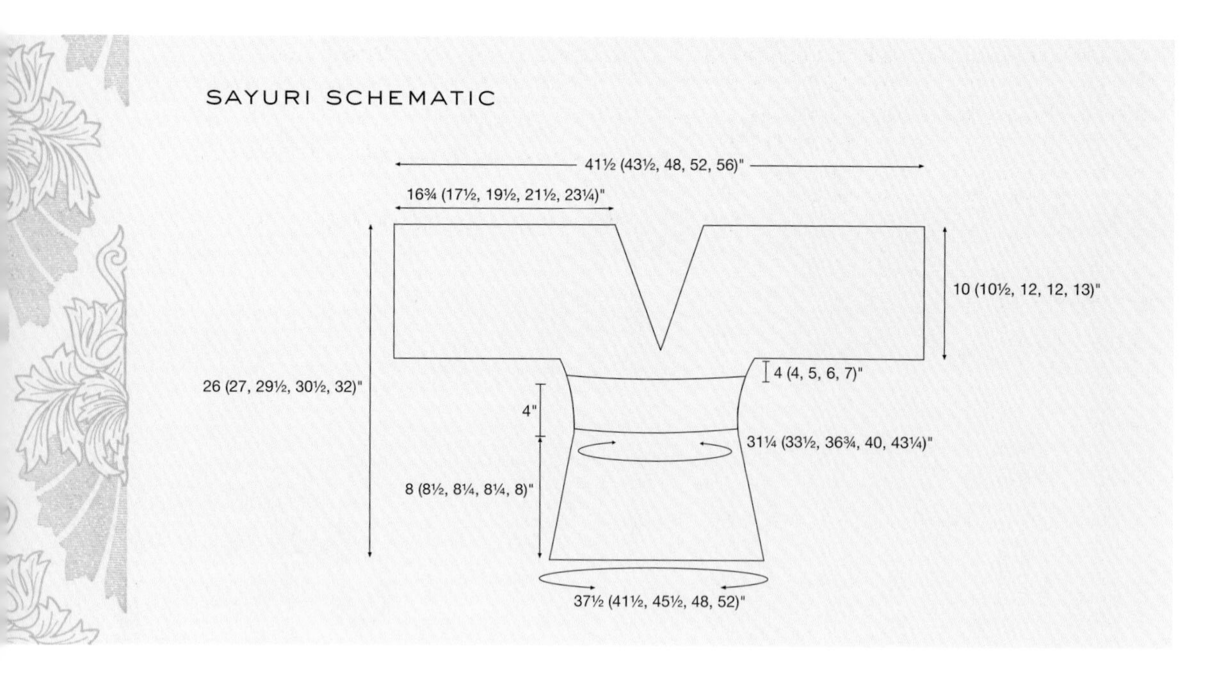

STITCH PATTERN

LINEN STITCH

(multiple of 2 sts; 4 rnds)

RND 1: *K1, yf, s1, yb; rep from * to end of rnd.

RNDS 2 AND 4: Knit.

RND 3: *Yf, s1, yb, k1; rep from * to end of rnd.

Rep Rnds 1–4.

BACK

Using provisional cast-on (see Special Techniques, page 137) and 5mm needles, CO 78 (84, 92, 100, 108) sts.

Work in St st for 15 (11, 13, 15, 19) rows, ending with WS row.

INC ROW (RS): K1, m1, knit to last 2 sts, m1, k1.

NEXT ROW (WS): Purl

Rep last two rows 4 (6, 8, 9, 10) more times—88 (98, 110, 120, 130) sts. Piece should measure 4 (4, 5, 6, 7)" from cast-on edge.

SLEEVES

Next row CO 60 (60, 65, 70, 75) sts using backward loop cast-on (see Special Techniques, page 137), knit to end. Turn work.

CO 60 (60, 65, 70, 75) sts in same manner, purl to end—208 (218, 240, 260, 280) sts.

Work even for 10 (11, 12, 12, 13)", ending with RS row.

NECK SHAPING

Purl 84 (88, 98, 107, 116) sts, BO center 40 (42, 44, 46, 48) sts, purl to end.

WORKING LEFT FRONT ONLY

Next row, k83 (87, 97, 106, 115) sts, m1, k1.

Inc every 3rd row at neck edge 19 (20, 21, 22, 23) more times—104 (109, 120, 130, 140) sts.

Work even for 0 (0, 6, 3, 6) rows.

Place sts on holder or scrap yarn. Break yarn.

RIGHT FRONT

With RS facing, join yarn at neck edge (after bound off sts). K1, m1, and knit to end.

Cont as for left front, reversing shaping, until fronts are same length.

Next RS row, knit across right front sts, then knit across left front sts, joining pieces to form V-neck.

Next row BO 60 (60, 65, 70, 75) sts, purl 88 (98, 110, 120, 130) sts, and BO 60 (60, 65, 70, 75) sts.

Rejoin yarn on RS to working sts.

DEC ROW: K2tog, knit to last 2 sts, k2tog.

Rep Dec Row EOR 4 (6, 8, 9, 10) more times—78 (84, 92, 100, 108) sts rem.

Work in St st for 16 (12, 14, 16, 20) rows, end with WS row.

Undo provisional cast-on and place back sts on needle to join in the rnd. Pm to indicate beg of rnd and knit 1 rnd—156 (168, 184, 200, 216) sts.

Beg Linen st and work for 4", (rep patt 12 times).

Next rnd k78 (84, 92, 100, 108), pm (this marks the halfway point in the rnd), knit to 1st before first marker, m1, k1, sm, m1, work to 1st before beg rnd marker, m1, k1, sm, m1 and work to end (4 sts inc). Work even for 4 rnds in St st. Rep last 5 rnds 7 (9, 10, 9, 7) more times—188 (208, 228, 240, 248) sts.

Knit 12 (6, 0, 0, 12) rnds or to desired length. For a longer sweater, cont in St st.

For hem turning ridge, purl next rnd.

Knit 5 more rnds.

BO all sts.

FINISHING

Sew side and sleeve seams. Fold hem under and sew to inside.

I-CORD EDGING

With 4.5mm dpns, CO 3 sts. Beg at back neck edge and with WS facing, pick up 1 st, *slide all 4 sts to other end of needle, k3, k2tog, pick up another st. Rep from * around the entire neck, picking up enough sts so V-neck does not pucker. At the bottom of the "V", pick up extra sts so I-cord bends to proper shape.

Rep I-cord around sleeve edges, if desired, or simply allow to curl in.

Block to measurements and weave in ends.

transparency SWEATER

véronique haegeli

The clean, elegant lines of Transparency are easily achieved with stockinette stitch in the round and without any seaming. Both the shaping, via darts, and the stretchiness of the thread-thin yarn will ensure a va-va-voom fit. The play on transparency is done simply by knitting using either one or two strands of yarn. But don't be fooled—the light-as-a-feather mohair/silk yarn will keep you warm! Delicate, rounded buttons add a fashionable flair as well as an interesting visual detail.

SIZES

XS (S, M, L, XL)

28–30 (32–34, 36–38, 40–42, 44–46)"

Shown in size S

FINISHED MEASUREMENTS

CHEST: 30 (34, 37½, 42, 46)"

LENGTH: 23½ (24, 24¼, 24½, 24¾)"

YARN

ShibuiKnits Silk Cloud (60% mohair, 40% silk; 330 yards/25g): 5 (5, 6, 6, 7) skeins, Pagoda (sc-181)

NEEDLES

3.5mm circular, 24" long

3.5mm dpns

NOTIONS

20 round ¼" buttons

Tapestry needle

Scrap yarn

Stitch markers in contrasting colors

GAUGE

20 sts and 36 rows = 4" in St st (after blocking)

pattern notes

Stockinette in this yarn is very stretchy, just like lace. To get an accurate gauge, measure after blocking.

Most of this design is knit using two strands of yarn. The yoke and the sleeve cuffs are knit using one strand of yarn to achieve a sheer effect.

Use markers in contrasting colors to distinguish between "dart markers" and those for side seams.

Véronique learned to knit from her grandmother. She left her native France for New York City just in time for the knitting boom. She is now pursuing a career as a neuroscientist by day and a knitting designer by night. You can follow her knitting adventures at treschicveronique.blogspot.com.

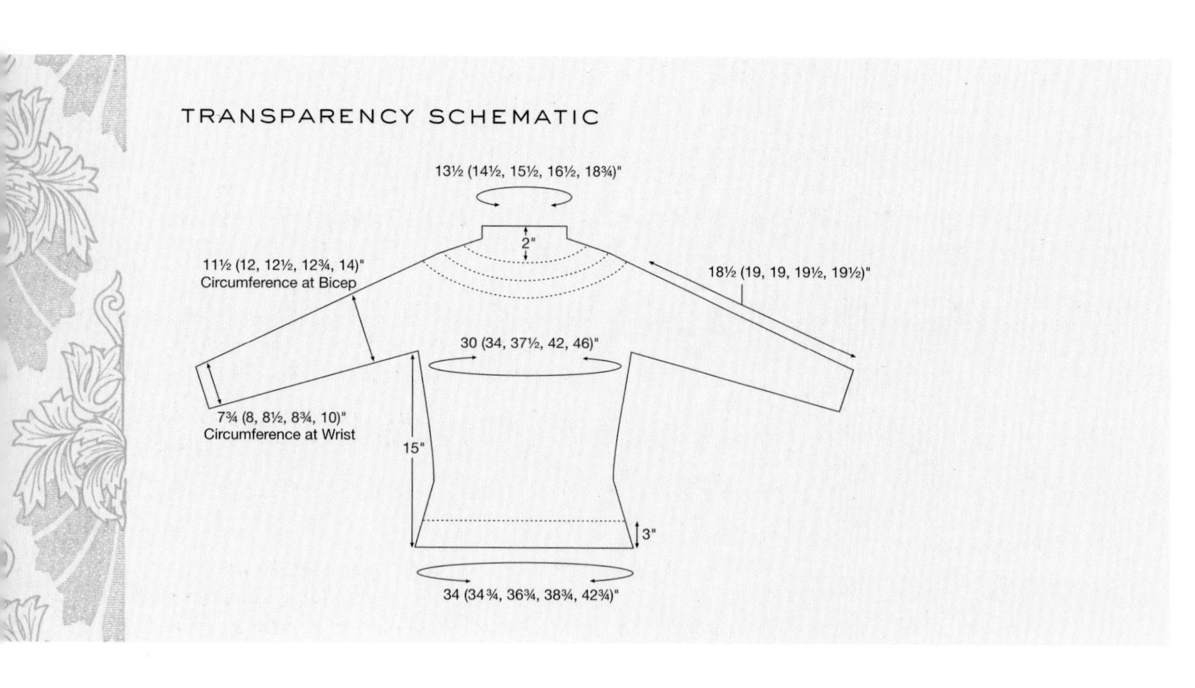

BODY

HEM

With 2 strands of yarn, work an I-cord cast-on over 170 (174, 184, 194, 214) st.

I-CORD CAST-ON: CO 3 st. K those 3 st.

*Place 3 st from RH needle to LH needle. K1fb of first st, then k2.

Rep from * until desired number of sts plus 2. Slide 3 sts from RH needle to LH needle. K2tog, k1. Slide 2 sts from RH needle to LH needle. K2tog.

Join for working in the rnd, being careful not to twist sts. Pm to indicate beg of rnd.

BODY

Place two markers, one at beg of rnd, and one after 85 (87, 92, 97, 107) sts, for side seams.

Work even for 3", placing additional markers (in contrasting colors) for bust darts on last rnd as foll:

*K25 (25, 27, 29, 32), pm, k35 (37, 38, 39, 43), pm, knit to side marker; rep from * around to beg of rnd.

WAIST SHAPING

DEC RND: *Work to 2 sts before first dart marker, k2tog, knit to 2nd dart marker, sm, ssk, knit to side seam marker; rep from * to beg of rnd.

Work even for 2 (3, 3, 4, 4) rnds.

Rep last 3 (4, 4, 5, 5) rnds 12 (10, 10, 8, 9) more times—118 (130, 140, 158, 174) sts rem.

Work even for 1".

BUST SHAPING

INC RND: work to first dart marker, M1R, sm, knit to second dart marker, sm, M1L, knit to side marker; rep from * to beg of rnd.

Work even for 6 (5, 4, 4, 3) rnds.

Rep last 7 (6, 5, 5, 4) rnds 7 (8, 11, 11, 13) more times—150 (170, 188, 210, 230) sts.

Work even until body measures 14½ (15, 15¼, 15½, 15¾)" from cast-on edge, end last rnd 7 (7, 7, 7, 8) sts before beg of rnd marker.

ARMHOLE SET-UP

Arrange underarm sts as foll:

Place next 14 (14, 14, 15, 16) sts on scrap yarn or st holders with side seam marker at center. Leave 68 (71, 80, 90, 99) sts on needle for front, place next 14 (14, 14, 15, 16) sts on scrap yarn or st holders, and leave 68 (71, 80, 90, 99) sts on needle for back. Set aside; beg sleeves.

SLEEVES (MAKE 2)

With one strand of yarn, work an I-cord cast-on over 38 (40, 42, 44, 50) sts. Join for working in the rnd, being careful not to twist sts, pm to indicate beg of rnd.

Work even for 1".

INC RND: K1, M1L, knit to last st, M1R, k1.

Work even for 11 rnds.

Rep last 12 rnds 9 times more—58 (60, 62, 64, 70) sts and, AT THE SAME TIME, when sleeve measures 5" from cast-on edge, begin knitting with 2 strands of yarn.

Work even until sleeve measures 18½ (19, 19, 19½, 19½)" from cast-on edge, ending last rnd 7 (7, 7, 7, 8) sts before beg of rnd marker.

Place next 14 (14, 14, 15, 16) sts on scrap yarn, with marker at center—44 (46, 48, 49, 54) sts rem for sleeve.

YOKE

Arrange sts on working needle for Yoke as foll (set-up rnd): sts for first sleeve (excluding underarm sts on holder), front sts, pm for neck opening, sts for second sleeve, and back sts—224 (234, 256, 278, 306) sts. Join for working in the rnd.

With one strand of yarn, work even for 3 rnds.

NECK OPENING

Work to marker (or desired point) for neck opening, turn work. Create opening by working back and forth instead of in the rnd. Work buttonholes at beg every 6th RS row as foll: K3, yo, k2tog. Cont in St st, working even for 4".

DEC ROW #1: *K2, k2tog; rep from * to end of round. End with — (k2, —, k2, k2)—168 (176, 192, 209, 230) sts rem.

Work even for 9 rows.

DEC ROW #2: *K1, k2tog; rep from * to end. End with — (k2, —, k2, k2)—112 (118, 128, 140, 154) sts rem.

DEC ROW #3: *K1, k2tog, k2tog; rep from * to end. End with k2 (k3, k3 —, —)—68 (72, 78, 84, 94) sts rem.

Work even for 19 rows, or desired collar height.

Bind off using I-cord bind-off.

FINISHING

Sew underarm seams. Weave in ends.

Block. Sew buttons opposite buttonholes for collar, and along the sleeve cuff.

ramona SWEATER

jared flood

SIZES

XS (S, M, L, XL)

28–30 (32–34, 36–38, 40–42, 44–46)"

Shown in size S

FINISHED MEASUREMENTS

CHEST: 30 (34, 38, 42, 46)"

YARN

Laines Du Nord "Cash-Silk" (50% extrafine merino, 25% silk, 25% cashmere; 67 yards/25g): 13 (15, 19, 23, 27) balls, Chocolate (8)

NEEDLES

4.5mm circulars, 32" long

4.5mm dpns

3.75mm circulars, 32" long

3.75mm dpns

NOTIONS

Tapestry needle

Stitch markers

Scrap yarn

GAUGE

20 sts and 30 rows = 4" in St st

Luxurious fiber blends demand equally elegant design ideas. Ramona combines classic elegance with clean comfort. Dress it up at the office or slip it on for a snuggly, sunlit day indoors. This design focuses on clean, form-fitting lines and comfortable sophistication utilizing the luxurious drape and hand of the cashmere/silk/merino blend fibers. With a deep V-neck, slightly belled sleeves, and a reverse center seam, Ramona will add a little excitement to your wardrobe while still crossing over into your everyday wear.

pattern notes

This pullover is worked top down with cast-on edge beginning at the top of the collar. After completing the shaping of the raglan yoke, you will put the sleeve stitches on scrap yarn and continue knitting the body back and forth in one piece. Worked like a cardigan in the round, Ramona is virtually seamless, aside from the center reverse-seam and the grafting of the underarms.

Hems on both sleeves and body are turned and sewn down to create a more sophisticated, elegant, and professional appearance.

Jared is an artist, photographer, and knitwear designer living and working in Brooklyn, New York. His designs have appeared in the most recent Stitch 'n Bitch *book as well as* Interweave Knits. *He tracks his fiber-related exploits at www.brooklyntweed.net.*

RAMONA SCHEMATICS

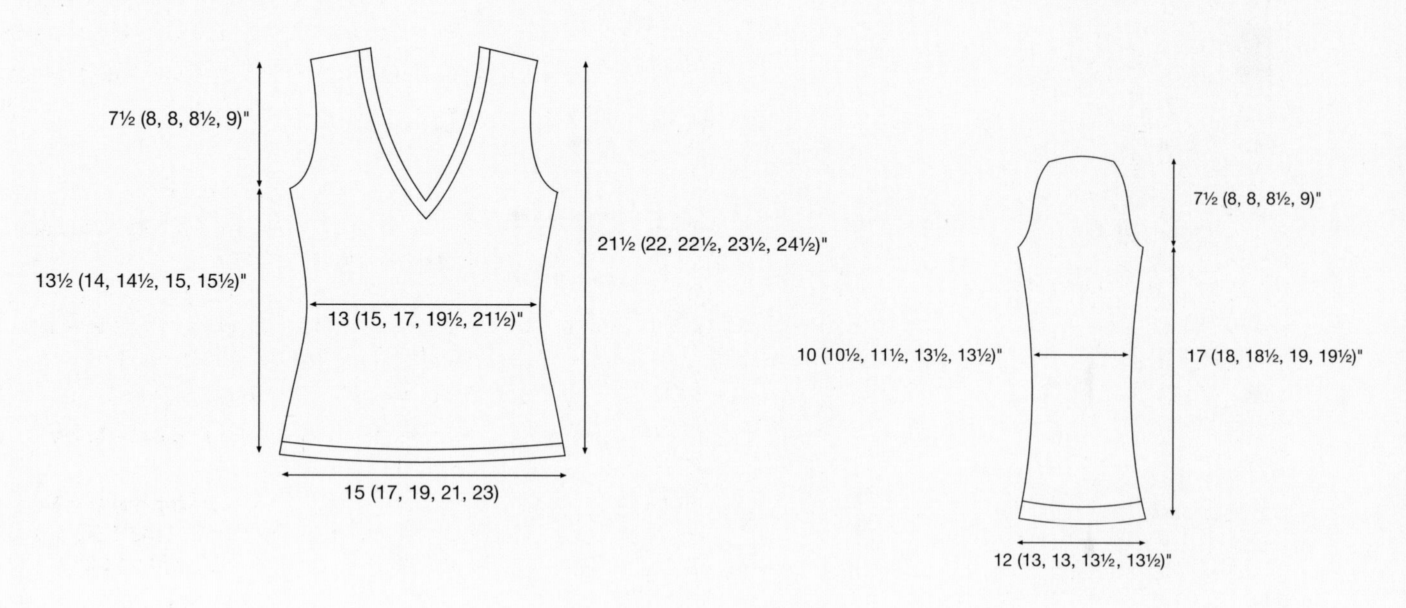

BODY

Using 4.5mm circular needle, CO 2 (2, 3, 2, 2), pm, CO 11 (12, 11, 13, 14), pm, CO 30 (34, 36, 36, 40), pm, CO 11 (12, 11, 13, 14), pm, CO 2 (2, 3, 2, 2)—56 (63, 64, 66, 72) sts.

ROW 1 AND ALL WS ROWS: Purl all sts.

ROW 2: *Knit to 1 st before marker, k1fb, sm, k1fb; rep from * 3 more times, knit to end of row.

INC ROW (ROW 4): K1, m1, *knit to 1 st before marker, k1fb, sm, k1fb; rep from * 3 more times, knit to last st, m1, k1.

Cont in St st, rep last 4 rows until 42 (50, 64, 80, 92) sts rem between back markers (#2 and #3).

Rep Inc Row 4 every 4th row 8 (10, 8, 6, 4) times until 58 (70, 80, 90, 100) sts rem between back markers (#2 and #3).

SIZE XS ONLY

ROW 1 (WS): Sl first st, m1, purl to last st, m1, sl last st.

ROW 2 (RS): Knit all sts.

ROW 3: Sl first st, purl to last st, sl last st.

ROW 4: Knit all sts.

SIZE S ONLY

ROW 1 (WS): Purl all sts.

ROW 2 (RS): Knit all sts.

ROW 3: Purl all sts.

ROW 4: K1, m1, knit to last st, m1, k1.

ALL SIZES

Work body setup row as follows:

Slip 1 (1, 1, 1, 0) st, inc 0 (1, 1, 1, 0) st(s). Purl to marker #1, sl all sts between markers #1 and #2 onto scrap yarn or holder, remove markers. CO 7 sts, pm, CO 7 sts, purl to marker #3. Sl all sts between markers #3 and #4 onto scrap yarn or holder. CO 7, pm, CO 7 sts, purl to last st, inc 0 (1, 1, 1, 0) st, sl 1 (1, 1, 1, 0) st.

SIZE XL ONLY

ROW 1: K all sts.

ROW 2: P all sts.

ROW 3: K1, m1, knit to last st, m1, k1.

ROW 4: Sl first st, m1, purl to last st, m1, sl last st.

SWEATER BODY

Beg body—150 (170, 190, 210, 230) sts on needle.

ROW 1: Knit all sts.

ROW 2: Sl first st, purl to last st, sl last st.

Rep last two rows 1 (2, 4, 8, 8) more time(s), ending with WS row.

WAIST SHAPING

Work one Dec Row as foll:

DEC ROW (RS): *Knit to 3 sts before underarm marker, ssk, k2, k2tog; rep from * one time, knit to end of rnd—146 (166, 186, 206, 226) sts rem.

Work as established in St st, slipping first and last st every WS row. Work a Dec Row every 10th (9th, 9th, 13th, 12th) row 4 (4, 4, 3, 3) more times—130 (150, 170, 194, 214) sts.

Work 9 (10, 10, 14, 14) rows even in St st, slipping first and last sts of WS rows and ending with WS row.

Work one Inc row as follows:

INC ROW (RS): *Knit to 1 st before underarm marker, m1, k1, sm, k1, m1; rep from * one time, knit to end of rnd—134 (154, 174, 198, 218) sts.

Work Inc Row every 10 (9, 9, 13, 12) rows 4 (4, 4, 3, 3) more times—150 (170, 190, 210, 230) sts.

Work as established until piece measures 13½ (14, 14, 14½, 15½)" from underarm, ending with RS row. Mark this final row with a coilless pin or removable st marker.

Switch to 3.75mm needles.

(WS) P1, p2tog, purl to last 3 sts, p2tog, p1.

Work in St st (not slipping first and last sts of WS rows) for 6 rows. Leave sts on needle. Fold hem along marked turn line and seam to inside of body.

Seam front of body together along slipped selvage edge, with selvage st facing out to create a reverse seam (refer to photo).

SLEEVES (MAKE 2)

Using 4.5mm dpns, evenly distribute sleeve sts from scrap yarn over needles.

Starting at beg of row, knit all sts. At end of row, CO 7 sts, pm, CO 7 sts (underarm). Join sleeve into rnd—54 (62, 70, 82, 90) sts on needle.

Work even for 25 (11, 9, 10, 5) rnds.

Work Dec Rnd as follows: K1, k2tog, k to last 3 sts, ssk, k1.

Continue knitting all rnds, working one Dec Rnd every 18th (10th, 10th, 8th, 6th) rnd 1 (4, 6, 7, 11) more time(s)—50 (52, 56, 66, 66) sts rem.

Knit 12 (9, 13, 10, 10) rnds even.

Work Inc Rnd as foll: K1, m1, knit to last st, m1, k1.

Continue knitting all sts and working an Inc Rnd as above every 13 (10, 15, 0, 0) rows, 4 (6, 3, 0, 0) more times—60 (66, 66, 68, 68) sts on needle.

Work even until sleeve measures 17½ (18, 18½, 19, 19½)" from underarm. Mark this final row with a coilless pin or removable st marker.

Switch to 3.75mm dpns.

Knit 6 rnds. Finish hem as for sweater body.

NECKBAND

Starting at right back neck, pick up 30 (35, 36, 37, 39) sts across back of neck, 10 (11, 11, 13, 14) sts across top of left sleeve, 38 (41, 44, 47, 50) sts down left front-neck, 1 st at center neck (just above center seam), mark center st with coilless pin or removable st marker. Continue picking up 38 (41, 44, 47, 50) sts up right front neck, 10 (11, 11, 13, 14) sts across top of right sleeve. Pm and join work—127 (140, 147, 158, 168) sts total.

Purl to within two sts of center marked st. P2tog, purl center st, p2togtbl, purl to end of rnd. Repeat last rnd one time.

BO in purl.

FINISHING

Block piece and pin to measurements. Steam hems flat. Weave in all ends.

multiplicity SWEATER

modalura: rachel chaffee and lucinda snyder

SIZES

XS (S, M, L, XL)

28–30 (32–34, 36–38, 40–42, 44–46)"

Shown in size M

FINISHED MEASUREMENTS

CHEST: 31½ (33½, 37, 39, 40)"

LENGTH: 27 (27, 27, 28, 28)"

YARN

YARN A: Fable Handknits (100% pure baby alpaca; 145 yards/50g): 6 (6, 6, 7, 8) skeins, Grey (17)

YARN B: Blue Sky Alpaca Brushed Suri (67% baby suri, 22% merino, 11% bamboo; 142 yards/50g):1 skein, Fudgesicle (604)

NEEDLES

4.5mm straight

NOTIONS

Six 1" buttons

Tapestry needle

GAUGE

22 sts and 32 rows = 4" in St st

This sweater can be worn four different ways. The long shoulder piece can be wrapped and buttoned tightly around the neck, loosely around the neck (like a cowl), gently across the waist and buttoned, or tossed casually over the left shoulder. The sweater is ribbed at the bottom and sleeve edges and accented with topstitching, giving this classic shape a deconstructed and modern look. Worked in Stockinette stitch, it will appeal to knitters of all levels. The body of the sweater is a neutral color, leaving room to play with color combinations for the topstitching.

pattern notes

Work selvage stitch on each edge of all pieces. Selvage stitches are included in the stitch count. It may be helpful to place a marker after the first stitch and before the last stitch.

ROW 1 (RS): Sl first st as if to knit, work across row and purl the last st.

ROW 2 (WS): Sl first st as if to knit, work across row, purl the last st.

Unless otherwise noted, all increases and decreases are worked as follows:

Ssk or k2tog worked 1 or 2 sts in from edges instead of immediate beginning or end of row.

The first half of Modalura is Lucinda Snyder, founder and owner of Wild Wools in Rochester, New York. The second half is Rachel Chaffee, who designs and sews clothing and accessories, both in shops across the U.S. and on her Web site, MadeByRachel.com. Lucinda and Rachel joined their talents in 2006 and the design team Modalura was born.

MULTIPLICITY SCHEMATICS

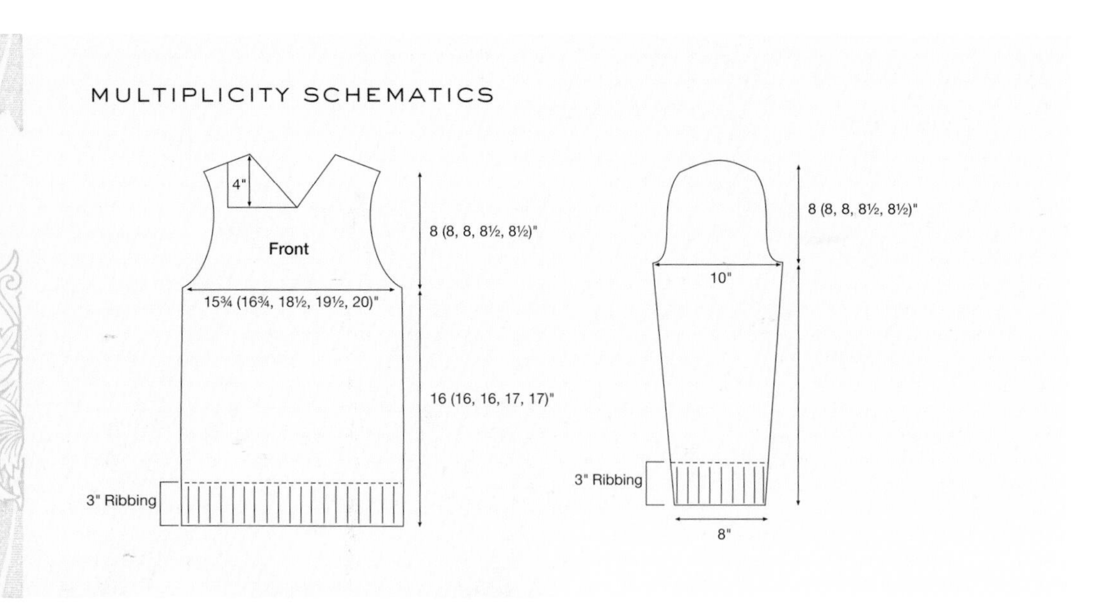

BACK

HEM

With Yarn A, CO 87 (92, 102, 107, 115) sts.

Work in k3, p2 rib until work measures 3" from cast-on edge.

Begin working in St st until piece measures 12 (12, 12, 13, 13)" from cast-on edge.

Next row (RS): Dec 1 st at each end every 7th row 4 times.

Continue to work in St st until piece measures 19 (19, 19, 20, 20)" from cast-on edge—79 (84, 94, 99, 111) sts.

SHAPE ARMHOLE

At beg of next 2 rows, BO 5 sts, then 3 sts.

Dec 1 st each end every RS row 4 times—55 (60, 70, 75, 87) sts.

Work even until armhole measures 8 (8, 8, 8½, 8½)" from cast-on edge.

SHAPE SHOULDER

At beg of next 2 rows BO 6 (6, 7, 7, 8) sts, then at beg of next 4 rows BO 6 sts—19 (24, 32, 37, 47) sts.

BO rem sts.

FRONT

Work as for back until armhole measures 6½ (6½, 6½, 7¾)", ending with a WS row.

Divide for neck and work each shoulder separately as foll:

Work across 18 (18, 19, 19, 20) sts. Attach second ball of yarn, BO the center 19 (24, 32, 37, 47) sts and work the rem 18 (18, 19, 19, 20) sts.

Work even until armhole measures 8 (8, 8, 8½, 8½)".

SHAPE SHOULDER

At armhole edges, BO 6 (6, 7, 7, 8) sts once, then 6 sts twice.

SLEEVES (MAKE 2)

Cast on 42 (42, 42, 42, 42) sts.

Work in k3, p2 rib until piece measures 3" from the cast-on edge.

Begin working in St st and AT THE SAME TIME inc 1 st each end every 20 rows 5 (5, 5, 6, 6) times—57 (57, 57, 59, 59) sts. Work even until piece measures 19 (19, 19, 20, 20)" or to desired length.

SHAPE CAP

At beg of next two rows, BO 3 sts, then dec 1 st each end every RS row 14 times—23 (23, 23, 25, 25) sts.

BO 4 sts at beg of next 2 rows.

BO rem 15 (15, 15, 17, 17) sts.

NECK (ALL SIZES)

Pick up 22 sts along right shoulder.

Working in St st, inc 1 st each end every 16 rows, 5 times—32 sts.

Then inc 1 st each end every 8 rows 11 times—54 sts.

Continue working in St st until piece measures 42" or desired length to go around the body.

On next RS row, begin working buttonholes as follows: K12, BO 3, k6, BO 3, k6, BO 3, k6, BO 3, k12.

On following row, purl all sts, casting on 3 sts in place of bound-off sts.

Work even for 4 rows. BO all sts.

FINISHING

Block pieces. Join shoulder seams and set in sleeves. Sew side and sleeve seams.

With Yarn B, pick up sts around neck and BO loosely on following row.

Using Yarn B, make a running st along both sides of sweater body and along neck pieces as well.

Sew buttons to left shoulder and along right side of the sweater.

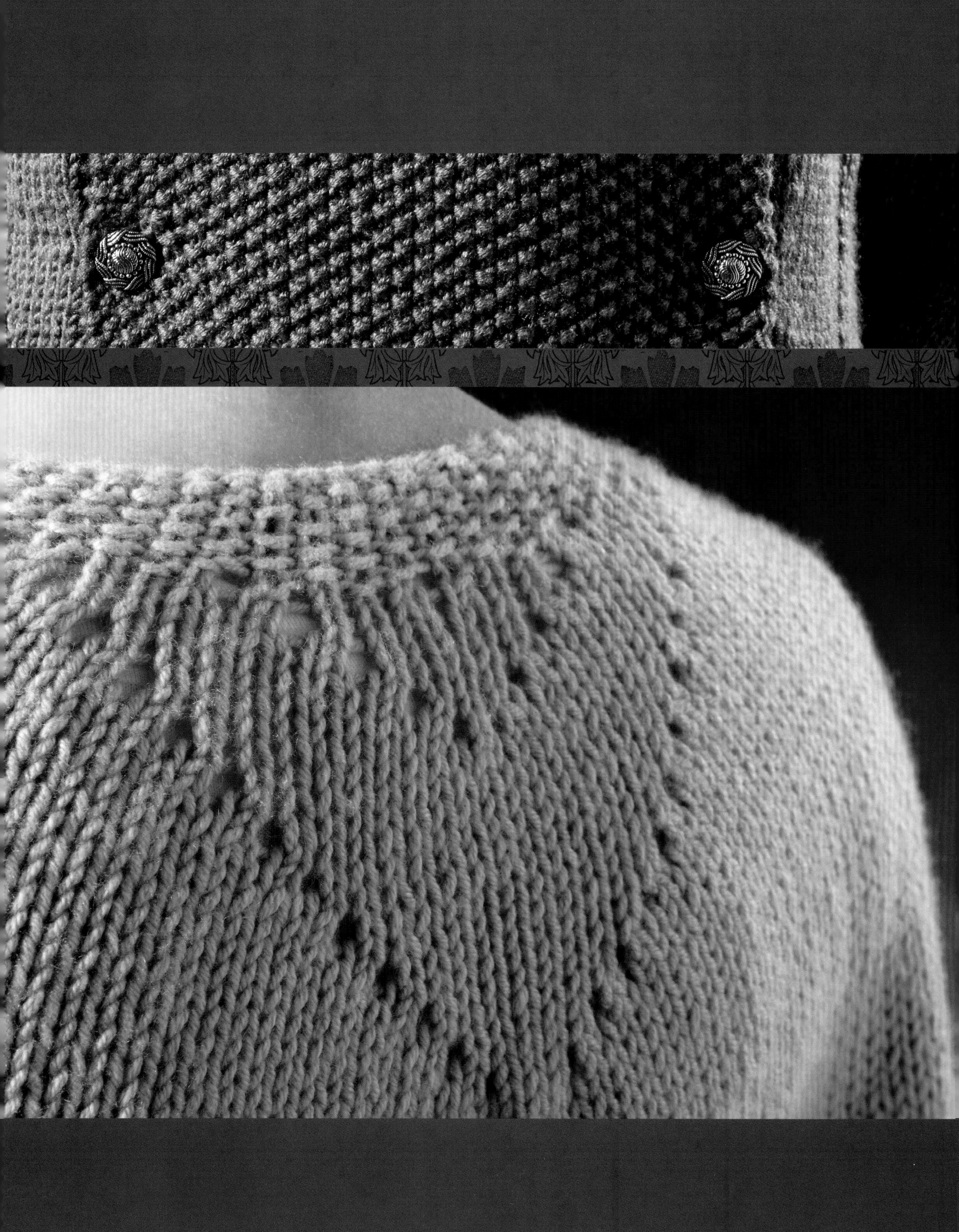

CHAPTER THREE

WRAPPED IN LUXURY

cardigans and jackets to keep you warm

joie de vivre CARDIGAN

véronique haegeli

Although Joie de Vivre looks very intricate with its lace upper portion, it is actually easy to make. The lower part is made in non-formfitting Garter rib, which creates vertical lines but does not pull in. The upper part is worked on the same number of stitches: it is looser only because of the lace stitch pattern! Joie de Vivre has an unusual construction: First you work the lower part in one piece, then you make each front and the back separately. Seam the sleeves and you are done!

SIZES

XS (S, M, L, XL)

UNDERBUST: 28 (30, 32, 34, 36)"

BUST: 28–30 (32–34, 36–38, 40–42, 44–46)"

Shown in size S

FINISHED MEASUREMENTS

unstretched

BUST: 33 (36, 38, 40, 42)"

LENGTH: 23½ (23½, 24, 24½, 24½)"

YARN

PureKnits Bamboo (100% bamboo; 220 yards/113g): 4 (5, 5, 5, 5) skeins, Red Light Special

NEEDLES

3.25mm circulars, 24" or 32" long

3.75mm circulars, 24" or 32" long

NOTIONS

One large button or shawl pin

Tapestry needle

Scrap yarn

GAUGE

20 sts and 28 rows = 4" in Garter rib with size 3.25mm needles

17 sts and 24 rows = 4" in Wavy Lace patt with size 3.75mm needles

pattern notes

Though the sweater is not knit in the round, circular needles are recommended to accommodate the large number of stitches.

The body of the sweater is knit in one piece in Garter rib up to the armholes. Then, the fronts and back are worked separately in Wavy Lace stitch pattern. Sleeves are integrated simply by casting on additional stitches.

In order to obtain a clean edging when working in Garter rib, slip the first stitch of each row with yarn in front, then move yarn to back. The slipped stitch is included in the stitch count.

Read instructions carefully before beginning; neckline decreases and sleeve increases are worked at the same time.

If sufficient stitches are not available for a full repeat of the lace pattern, continue in Garter rib as established.

Véronique learned to knit from her grandmother. She left her native France for New York City just in time for the knitting boom. She is now pursuing careers as a neuroscientist by day and a knitting designer by night. You can follow her knitting adventures at treschicveronique.blogspot.com.

STITCH PATTERNS

GARTER RIB

(multiple of 4 sts; 2-row repeat)

ROW 1 (AND ALL RS ROWS): Knit all sts.

ROW 2 (AND ALL WS ROWS): *K2, p2; rep from * to end.

WAVY LACE

(multiple of 8 sts; 12-row repeat)

ROW 1 (RS): *(P2, k1, yo, k1, p2, k1, drop st, k1); rep from * to end.

ROW 2 (AND ALL WS ROWS): Knit the knit sts and purl the purl sts.

ROWS 3, 5, 9 AND 11: Knit the knit sts and purl the purl sts.

ROW 7: *(P2, k1, drop st, k1, p2, k1, yo, k1); rep from * to end.

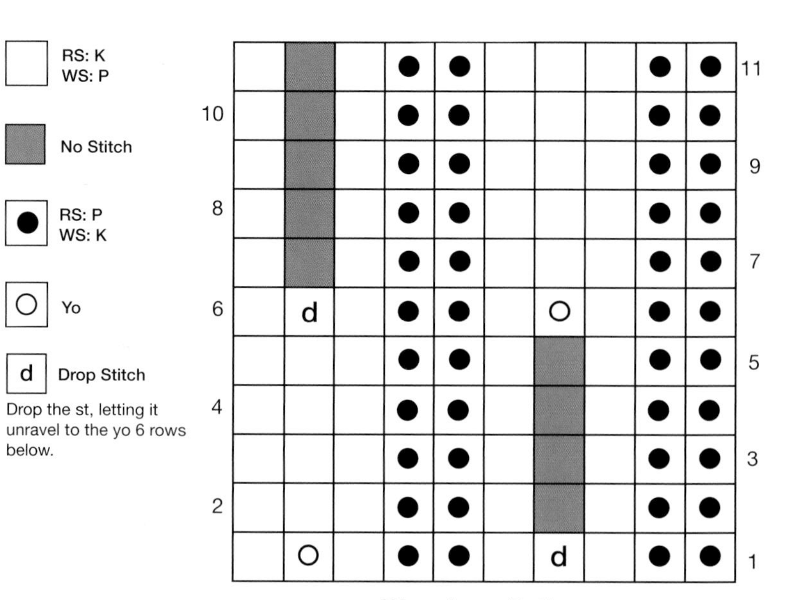

Wavy Lace Pattern

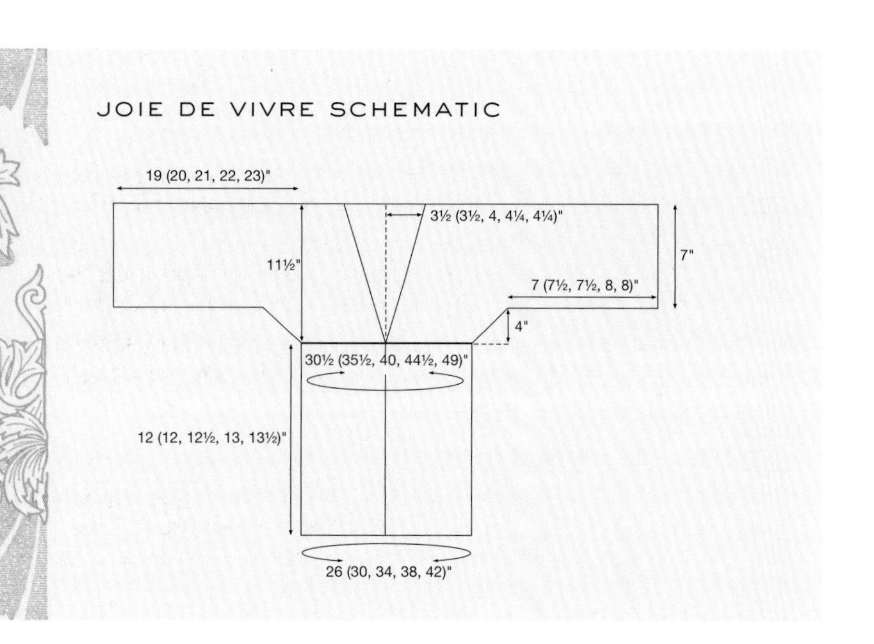

BODY

With smaller needles, CO 130 (150, 170, 190, 210) sts.

Work in Garter rib, making sure to begin and end each row with 2 sts in Garter st. Slip first st (selvage st) as indicated in Pattern Notes.

Work in Garter rib until piece measures 12 (12, 12½, 13, 13½)" from cast-on edge. Optional buttonhole row (RS) may be added here as foll:

K2, BO 2 sts, knit to end. On the next row (WS), cont in patt, CO 2 sts directly above bound-off sts, k2.

RIGHT FRONT

The right front is worked on the first 33 (38, 43, 48, 53) sts. Place rem 97 (112, 127, 142, 157) st on scrap yarn.

Neckline decreases will be introduced at beg of RS rows and AT THE SAME TIME, increases will be introduced at armhole (beg of WS rows) to form sleeves.

Switch to larger needle and work set-up row for right front with RS facing as foll: Maintain 2-st Garter edge, slipping the first st wyif, establish Wavy Lace patt: *(P2, k1, yo, k1, p2, k2); rep from * to end.

DEC ROW (RS): Slip first st, k1, ssk, continue in Wavy Lace patt as set.

Work *Dec Row every 4th row 3 (2, 7, 17, 17) times, then Dec Row every 6th row once*. Repeat from * to * 3 (5, 0, 0, 0) times. Then work Dec Row every 4th row 2 (0, 8, 0, 0) times, and work Dec Row every 6th row 1 (0, 1, 0, 0) time—68 (70, 72, 74, 74) rows worked, 15 (15, 17, 18, 18) sts decreased.

AT THE SAME TIME, on WS rows, using the cable cast-on method, CO 2 sts EOR 12 times.

On next RS row, CO 30 (32, 32, 34, 34) sts—54 (56, 56, 58, 58) sts increased overall.

After 68 (70, 72, 74, 74) rows have been worked, 72 (79, 82, 88, 93) sts rem. BO all sts.

LEFT FRONT

Place last 33 (38, 43, 48, 53) sts on working needle for left front. Keep rem 64 (74, 84, 94, 104) sts on scrap yarn for back.

Work as for right front, introducing neckline decs at end of RS rows and sleeve incs at beg of RS rows.

Maintain 2-st Garter edge as for right front, substituting dec row as foll (RS): Work in Wavy Lace patt to last 4 sts, k2tog, k2.

BACK

Place rem 72 (79, 82, 88, 93) sts on needle and work in Wavy Lace patt. Work sleeve incs on both sides as for fronts to form sleeves—150 (159, 162, 170, 175) sts total.

Work a total of 68 (70, 72, 74, 74) rows, or until sleeves are same length as for fronts. BO all sts.

FINISHING

Match sleeve fronts and backs. Sew top seams of sleeves together, then bottom seams. If desired, sew on button opposite buttonhole. Since the lace pattern is very stretchy, block it to obtain long, skinny sleeves, or shorter, wider sleeves.

rosamund MODERN KIMONO

stephanie degen

SIZES

S (M, L)

32–34 (36–38, 40–42)"

Shown in size M

FINISHED MEASUREMENTS

unstretched

CHEST: 38 (40, 44)"

HEM CIRCUMFERENCE: 46 (48, 52)"

LENGTH: 24½"

YARN

YARN A: Kaalund Yarns Silk-stralis (50% cultivated silk, 50% wool; 131 yards/50g): 9 (10, 12) skeins, Kingfisher

YARN B: Louisa Harding Grace (50% merino wool, 50% silk; 110 yards/50g): 2 skeins, Ecru (01)

NEEDLES

4mm circulars, 40" long

4mm circulars, 24" long,

NOTIONS

1" round button

Tapestry needle

GAUGE

20 sts and 24 rows = 4" in St st

Inspired by the fluid fashions of the 1930s, Rosamund is an elegant, kimono-inspired cardigan that looks lovely with either a dress or jeans. Fitted on top and flaring out towards the hips, this top-down knit can easily be altered to fit your specific measurements. Floral intarsia winding around the body creates a dramatic effect.

pattern notes

Jacket is worked top down flat on circular needles to accommodate large number of stitches. See Special Techniques (page 137) for hints on working intarsia.

Right sides of intarsia charts show actual distance from start of row, though not to end of row.

Stephanie learned to knit and crochet from her grandma and her elementary school. Having lived in Germany and Southern California, she now calls the Bay Area her home. There she works for a publishing company and freelances as a bookbinder.

SLEEVE CHART

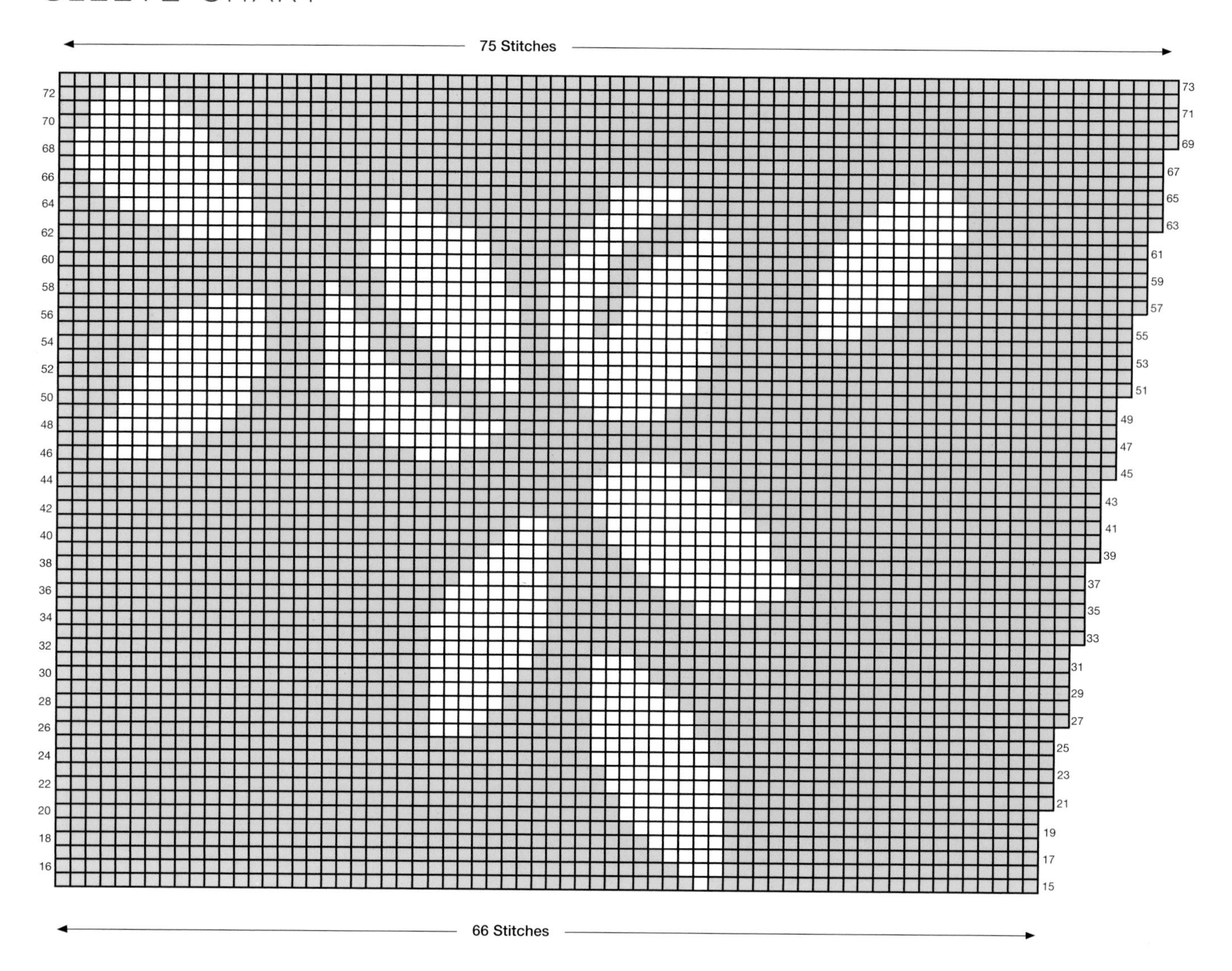

FRONT CHART

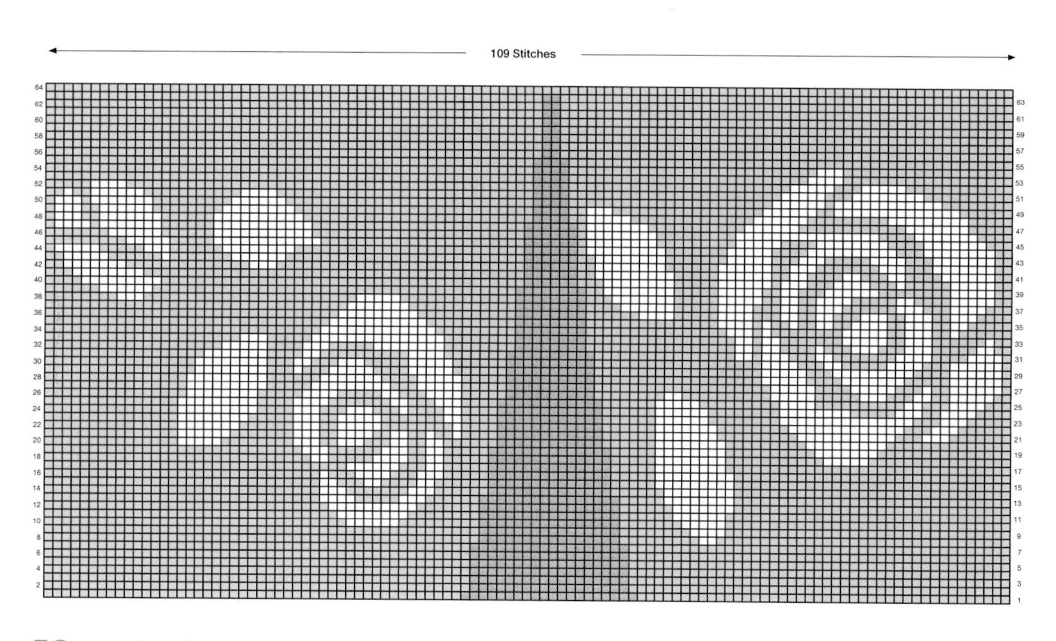

SHOULDER CHART

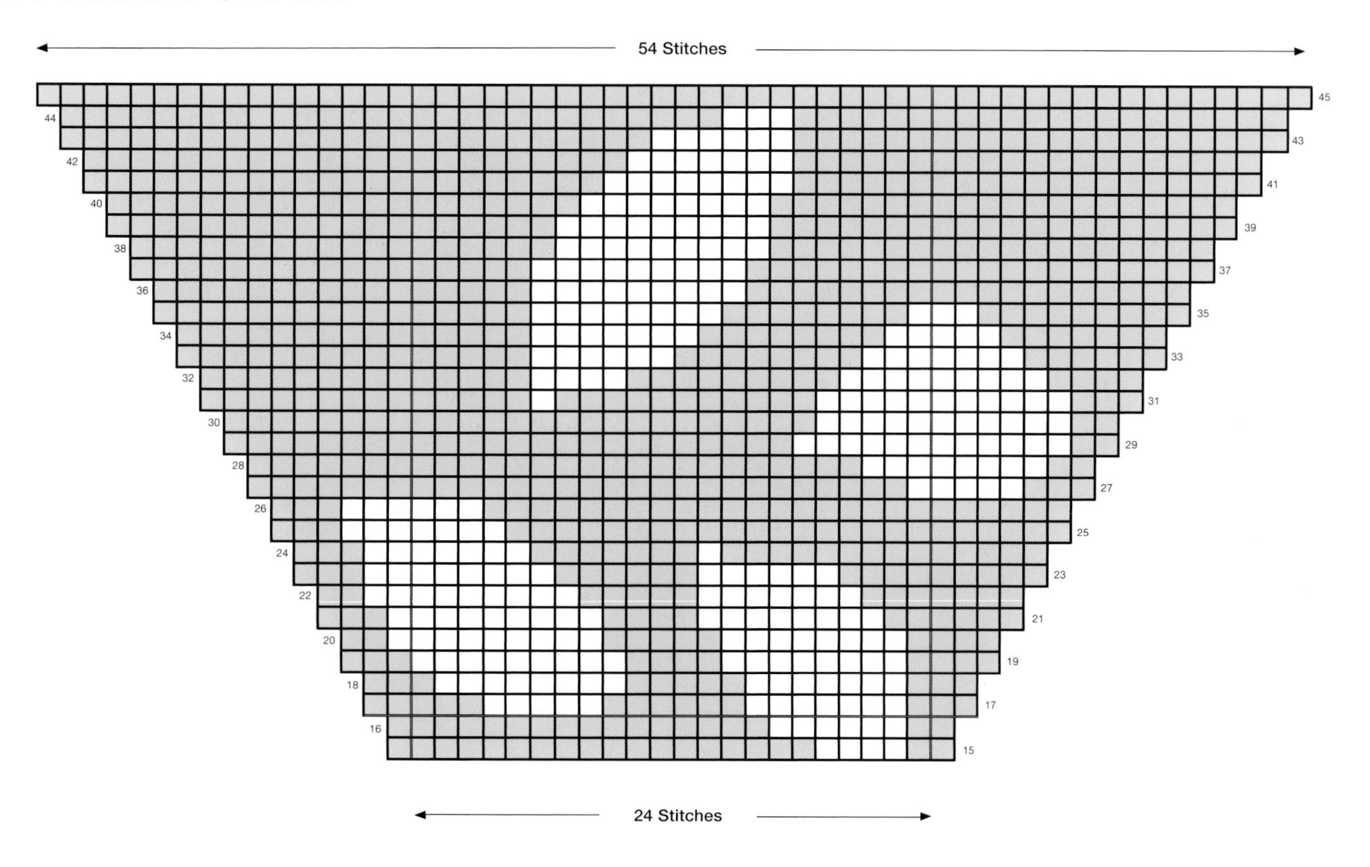

BACK CHART

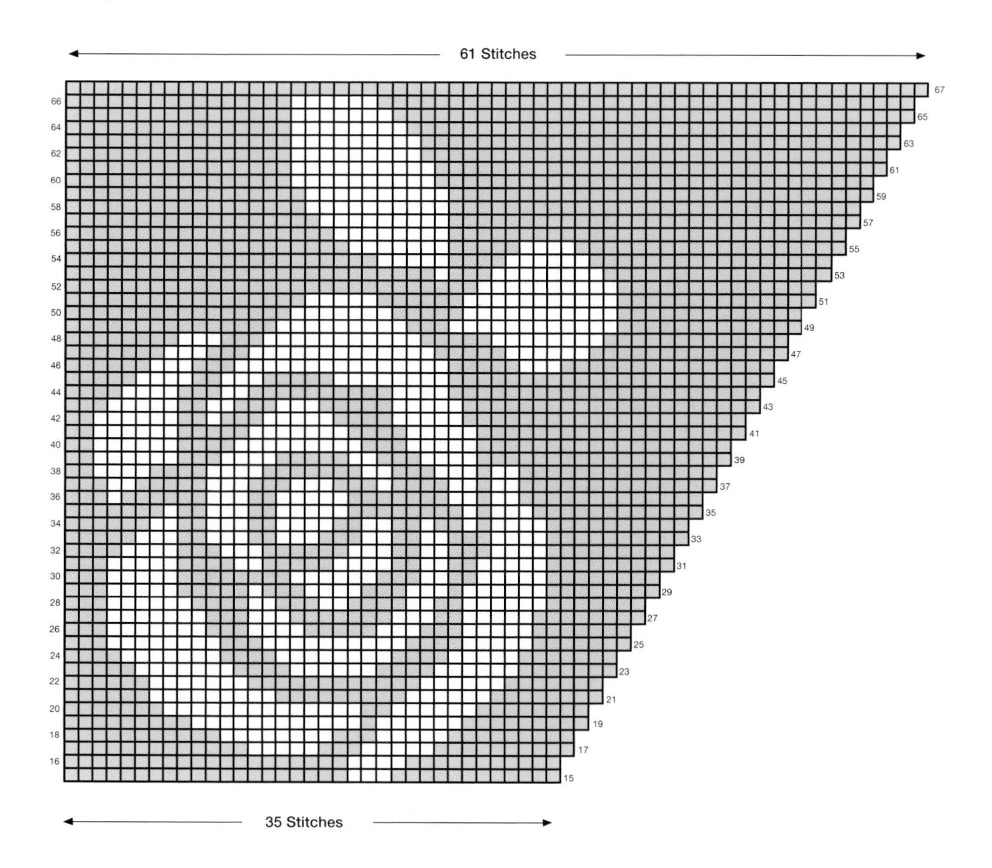

STITCH PATTERN

SEED STITCH

(multiple of 2 sts, 2-row repeat)

ROW 1: *K1, p1; rep from * to end.

ROW 2: *P1, k1; rep from * to end.

Rep Rows 1 and 2.

YOKE

With Yarn A and shorter needles, CO 50 (66, 66) sts.

ROW 1 (RS): Place markers as foll: K2 (4, 4) (left front), pm, k8 (10, 8) (left sleeve), pm, k30 (38, 42) (back), pm, k8 (10, 8) (right sleeve), pm, k2 (4, 4) (right front).

ROW 2 AND ALL EVEN ROWS (WS): Purl.

ROW 3, 5, 7: *Knit to 1 st before marker, k1fb, sm, k1fb; repeat from * four times, knit to end.

ROW 9: K2, m1, *k to 1 st before marker, k1fb, sm, k1fb; repeat from * four times, knit to last 2 sts, m1, knit to end.

ROW 11, 13, 15, 17: *Knit to 1 st before marker, k1fb, sm, k1fb; repeat from * four times, knit to end. On Row 15, work to second marker and begin intarsia Shoulder Chart, work to next marker, and begin Back Chart, work to end.

ROW 19: K2, m1, *k to 1 st before marker, k1fb, sm, k1fb; repeat from * four times, k to last 2 sts, m1, knit to end.

Repeat Rows 12–19, continuing m1 increases at left and right front edges every 10th row 5 (5, 6) more times until a total of 336 (352, 394) sts are on needles, ending with RS row—76 (78, 86) sts each for sleeves, 43 (45, 51) sts each for right and left front, and 98 (106, 120) sts for back.

Place sleeve sts on scrap yarn.

Purl right front sts, put right sleeve sts on holder, pm, purl back sts, put left sleeve sts on holder, pm, purl left front sts.

Continue in St st for 5".

Start side increases as foll:

INC ROW: *Knit to 2 sts before marker, m1, knit to marker, sm, k2, m1, knit to next marker; rep from *.

Rep Inc Row every 6th row 5 times more, then every 8th row 4 more times. AT THE SAME TIME, beg Front Chart on second Inc Row. After last increase, purl one row.

Work in Seed st for 10 rows. BO.

RIGHT SLEEVE

Transfer sts from holder to needle. Work in St st for 3½", ending with WS row.

INC ROW (RS): K2, m1, knit to last two sts, m1, knit to end.

Rep Inc Row every 6th row eight times more. Work in St st for 1", ending with WS row. Continue in Seed st for 10 rows. BO.

LEFT SLEEVE

Work as for right sleeve, beg Sleeve Chart on Row 16.

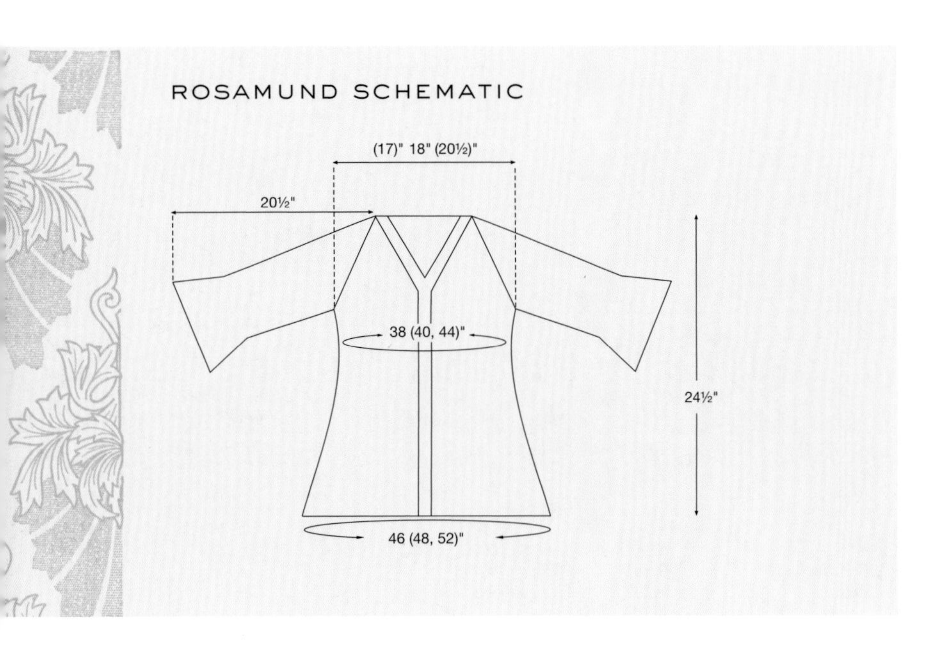

FRONT AND NECK BAND

With long needles and RS of work facing, start at hem edge and pick up 3 sts out of every 4 on front edge until cast-on edge. Pick up 1 st for every knitted st around neck. On other side of front edge, again pick up 3 sts out of every 4.

Work in Seed st for 10 rows adding buttonhole on right side just below bust on Row 5.

BUTTONHOLE ROW: Work in Seed st to desired location, BO 3 sts, work to end in Seed st. On foll row, CO 3 sts opposite bound-off sts, work end. BO.

FINISHING

Sew sleeve seams using mattress stitch (see Special Techniques, page 138). Weave in all ends. Jacket can either be blocked in pieces or steam blocked using a moist towel and medium heat dry iron. Sew button to left side front band opposite buttonhole.

seeded cables CARDIGAN

sarah heiniger

The soft, full cables of this design are accentuated by the Pear Tree Merino. The subtle color changes and tautness add to the texture of the piece. It also makes for a widely versatile garment. Wear it with a belt, a wide ribbon around the waist, over jeans, or to complement a skirt. Any way you flaunt it, the cables and shaping are sure to flatter.

SIZES

XS (S, M, L, XL, 2X)

28–30 (32–34, 36–38, 40–42, 44–46, 48–50)"

Shown in size XS

FINISHED MEASUREMENTS

unstretched

BUST: 14½ (16½, 18½, 20½, 22½, 24½)"

WAIST: 10½ (12½, 14½, 16½, 18½, 20½)"

HIPS: 15½ (17½, 19½, 21½, 23½, 25½)"

COLLAR TO HEM: 26 (26½, 26½, 27, 27, 27½)"

SLEEVE CIRCUMFERENCE (UPPER ARM): 11 (11½, 12, 12½, 13, 13½)"

YARN

Pear Tree 8-ply Merino (100% Australian merino wool; 107 yards/50g): 9 (9, 10, 10, 11, 11) skeins, Robin's Egg

NEEDLES

3.75mm circulars

NOTIONS

Stitch markers

Cable needle

Tapestry needle

Scrap yarn

GAUGE

20 sts and 32 rows = 4" in St st

pattern notes

Circular needles are not required, but are recommended to accommodate the large number of stiches.

The cardigan is very fitted, with shaping through the waist and hips. If you prefer a looser garment, knit a larger size.

The set-up rows for all cable patterns are wrong side rows. Read all charted set-up rows from left to right.

Sarah picked up a pair of knitting needles one day and has never looked back. She has always loved classic silhouettes and cables and so it just seemed natural that such a piece would be her first published work. She lives and works just outside of Chicago and archives her knitting progress on her blog, persnickety.blogspirit.com.

STITCH PATTERNS

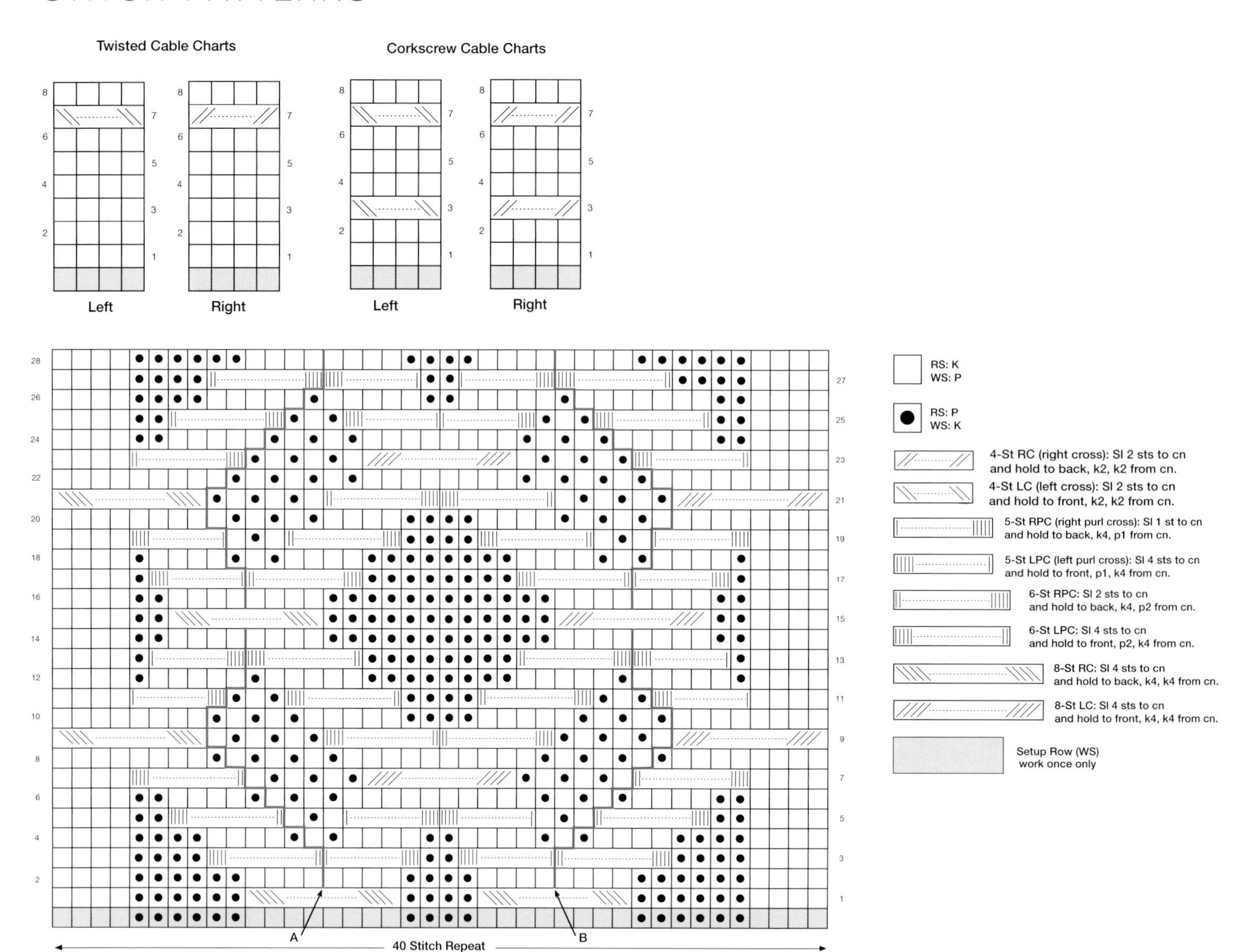

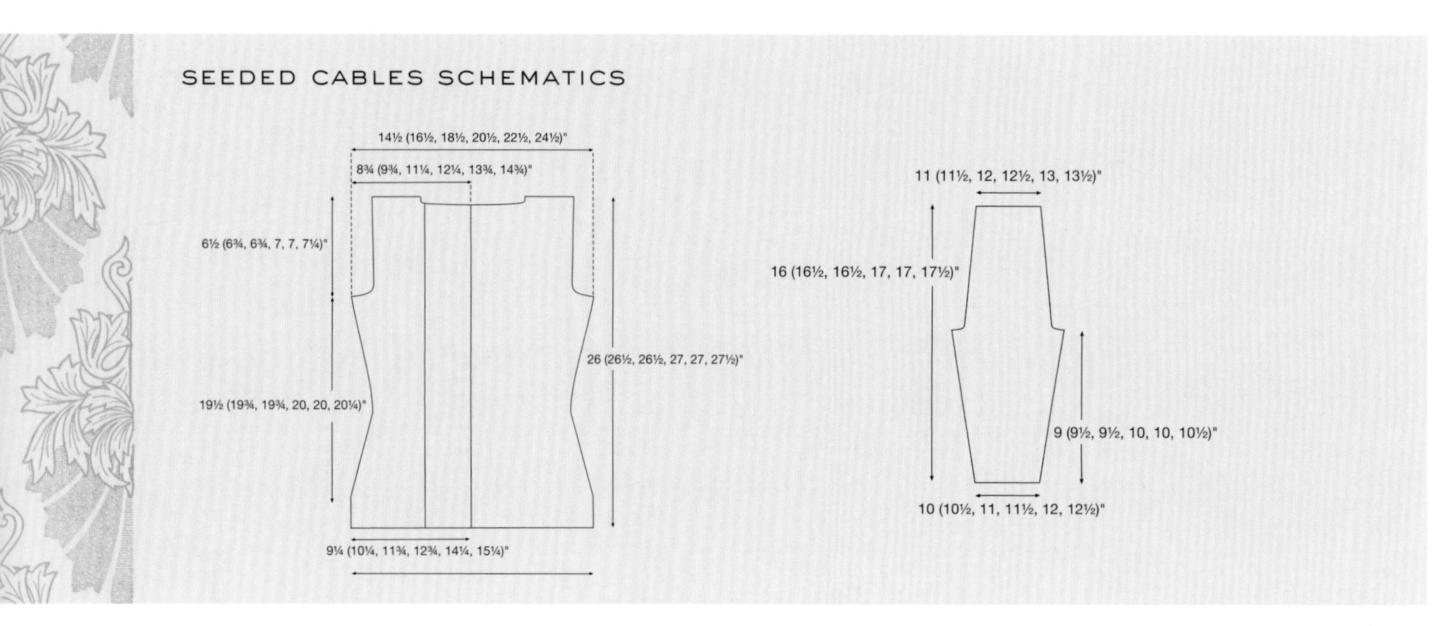

BACK

Using tubular cast-on, CO 94 (104, 114, 124, 134, 144) sts (see Special Techniques, page 137). On the next row, establish k2, p2 rib as foll:

Purl 1 st, *k1, put next st (purl st) on cable needle (cn) and hold to back of work. Knit next st from LH needle, purl st from cn. Purl next st. Rep from * to end of row.

SET UP PATTS

NEXT ROW (WS): P1 (selvage st), p2, k4 (9, 14, 19, 24, 29), pm, work left Corkscrew Cable set-up row over next 4 sts, pm, k2, p2, k2, pm, work left Twisted Cable set-up row over next 4 sts, pm, k2, p2, k2, pm, work Seeded Cable patt set-up row over next 40 sts, pm, k2, p2, k2, work right Twisted Cable set-up row over next 4 sts, pm, k2, p2, k2, pm, work right Corkscrew Cable set-up row over next 4 sts, pm, k4 (9, 14, 19, 24, 29), p2, p1 (selvage st).

WAIST SHAPING

Continue patt as set, and AT THE SAME TIME, dec 1 st each end Row 5 and every 4th row 2 more times as foll: K3, ssk, work to last 5 sts, k2tog, k3.

Work as set for 3 rows.

NEXT ROW: Work Chart Row 17: K3, p1, k2, ssk, cont as set to last 8 sts, k2tog, k2, p1, k3.

NEXT ROW (WS): Work as set.

NEXT ROW: Work Chart Row 19: K3, p1, sl 1 to cn, k2, k1 from cn, work as set to last 7 sts, sl 1 to cn, k2, k1 from cn, p1, k3.

NEXT ROW: Work as set.

NEXT ROW: Work Chart Row 21: K3, p1, k1, ssk, work as set to last 7 sts, k2tog, k1, p1, k3.

Work as set for 3 rows, ending WS row.

NEXT ROW: Work Chart Row 25: K3, ssk, work as set to last 5 sts, k2tog, k3.

Work as set for 3 rows, ending WS row.

NEXT ROW: Work Chart Row 1: K3, ssk, work as set to last 5 sts, k2tog, k3.

Work as set for 5 rows.

NEXT ROW: Work Chart Row 7: K2, ssk, work as set to last 4 sts, k2tog, k2.

Work as set for 5 rows.

NEXT ROW: Work Chart Row 13: K3, p2tog, work as set to last 5 sts, p2tog, k3.

Work as set for 13 (15, 15, 17, 17, 19) rows—76 (86, 96, 106, 116, 126) sts rem.

NEXT ROW: Work Chart Row 27 (1, 1, 3, 3, 5): K3, M1p, work as set to last 3 sts, M1p, k3.

Work as set for 7 rows.

NEXT ROW: Work Chart Row 7 (9, 9, 11, 11, 13) and foll 8th row 2 times: K1, M1L , k2, work as set to last st, M1R, k1.

Work as set for 7 rows.

NEXT ROW: Work Chart Row 3 (5, 5, 7, 7, 9): K1, M1L, k1, begin left Corkscrew Cable over next 4 sts, work as set to last 6 sts, work right Corkscrew Cable over next 4 sts, k1, M1R, k1.

Work as set for 7 rows.

NEXT ROW: Work Chart Row 11 (13, 13, 15, 15, 17) and foll 8th row 3 times: K3, m1 p, work as set to last 3 sts, m1 p, k3—94 (104, 114, 124, 134) sts.

Work as set for 15 rows.

ARMHOLE SHAPING

NEXT TWO ROWS: Work Chart Rows 23 (25, 25, 27, 27, 1) and 24 (26, 26, 28, 28, 2): BO first 8 (10, 12, 14, 16, 18) sts, k3, work as set to end of row—78 (84, 90, 96, 102, 108).

NEXT ROW: Work Chart Row 25 (27, 27, 1, 1, 3) and foll 4th row 2 times: Ssk, work as set to last 2 sts, k2tog.

Work 3 rows as set.

NEXT ROW: Work Chart Row 9 (11, 11, 13, 13, 15): P2tog, work as set to last 2 sts, p2tog.

Work as set for 27 (29, 29, 31, 31, 33) rows.

COLLAR SHAPING

NEXT ROW: Work Chart Row 7 (9, 9, 11, 11, 13): Work to marker for Seeded Cable patt, remove marker, k4 (3, 3, 2, 2, 1), BO next 25 (26, 26, 27, 27, 28) sts, k4 (3, 3, 2, 2, 1), remove marker, work to end of row.

NEXT ROW (WS): Work Chart Row 8 (10, 10, 12, 12, 14): Work as set to last 2 sts on left shoulder, ssk, join yarn to right shoulder at neck edge, k2tog, work as set.

NEXT ROW: Work Chart Row 9 (11, 11, 13, 13, 15) and foll 2 rows: Work as set to last 2 sts on right shoulder, k2tog, ssk first 2 sts of left shoulder, work as set to end of row—22 (26, 31, 36, 41, 46) sts each side. BO all rem sts.

RIGHT FRONT

Using tubular cast-on, CO 58 (63, 68, 73, 78, 83) sts. On the next row, establish k2, p2 rib as for back.

Start next row (WS): P1 (selvage st), p2, k12 (17, 22, 27, 32, 39), pm, work Seeded Cable patt set-up row, pm, k1, p1, p1 (selvage st).

Work the next row (RS) as foll: K2, p1, sm, work Row 1 of Seeded Cable, sm, p12 (17, 22, 27, 32, 39), k3.

WAIST SHAPING

Cont to work as set, and AT THE SAME TIME, starting on Row 5, dec 1 st at end every 4th row, 7 times, then every 6th row 2 times as foll: Work to last 5 sts, p2tog, k3—49 (54, 59, 64, 69, 74) sts rem.

Work as set for 13 (15, 15, 17, 17, 19) rows.

On the next row (row 27 (1, 1, 3, 3, 5) of chart) and every following 8th row 8 times, inc 1 st as foll: Work to last 3 sts, M1L, k3—57 (62, 67, 72, 77, 82) sts rem.

Work as set for 14 rows.

ARMHOLE SHAPING

On next WS row (chart row 22 (24, 24, 26, 26, 28)), BO first 8 (10, 12, 14, 16, 18) sts, work as set to end of row, then dec 1 st at armhole edge every 4th row 4 times, beg with chart row 27 (1, 1, 3, 3, 5).

Work as set for 27 (29, 29, 31, 31, 33) rows.

At beg of 7th patt rep, BO first 5 sts of row 1 (3, 3, 5, 5, 7). Maintain patt, dec 1 st at armhole edge every row four times. Work 1 WS row—36 (41, 46, 51, 56, 61) sts rem. Next RS row, BO all rem sts.

LEFT FRONT

Work as for right front, establishing set-up row as foll (WS): P1 selvage st, p1, k1, pm, work Seeded Cable patt set-up row, pm, k12 (17, 22, 27, 32, 39), p2, p1 (selvage st). Reverse all shaping, substituting M1R for M1L on Inc Rows.

SLEEVES (MAKE 2)

Using the tubular cast-on, CO 56 (59, 62, 65, 68, 71) sts.

NEXT ROW (WS): P2, k2, p2, k2, pm, work Seeded Cable set-up row, pm, k2, p2, k2, p2.

NEXT ROW (RS): Work as set. AT THE SAME TIME, inc 1 st on both ends every 12th (12th, 12th, 13th, 13th, 14th) row 6 times—68 (71, 74, 77, 80, 83) total sts. Work 7 more rows, then BO the first 8 sts on next 2 rows—52 (55, 58, 61, 64, 67) sts rem.

SLEEVE CAP

Work 14 (18, 18, 22, 22, 26) rows as set. Work decs for sleeve cap as foll:

NEXT ROW: Work Row 16 (20, 20, 24, 24, 28) of Seeded Cable chart: Work to 2 sts before marker, p2tog, sm, Seeded Cable patt, sm, p2tog, work to end of row.

Work 6 rows as set.

DEC ROW (RS): Work to 2 sts before marker, k2tog, sm, Seeded Cable patt, sm, ssk, work to end of row.

Rep Dec Row every 4 rows 2 times, then EOR 3 times.

NEXT ROW: Work Row 9 (13, 13, 17, 17, 21) of Seeded Cable chart: Dec one st at each end of work as established. AT THE SAME TIME, from this row onward, only work between A and B on Seeded Cable Chart; work rem pattern sts as set.

Work Dec Row EOR 1 more time, then every row 1 time.

Maintaining patt, BO 3 sts at beg of next 2 rows, then 4 sts at beg of next 2 rows.

BO all rem sts—18 (21, 24, 27, 30, 33) sts.

FINISHING

Completely wet all pieces and pin to specified measurements. Allow to dry completely. Join shoulder seams using mattress stitch (see Special Techniques, page 137). Set in sleeves, sew side seams. Work front ribbing and collar as foll:

FRONT PLACKET

On right front and beg at cast-on edge, pick up and knit 169 (177, 177, 185, 185, 185) sts along center edge (RS). P3, *k2, p2; rep from * to end of row. Work as set for 12 (16, 16, 20, 20, 24) more rows or until rib measures 1½ (2, 2, 2½, 2½, 3)". BO in knit.

On left front and beg at neck edge, pick up and knit 169 (177, 177, 185, 185, 185) sts along inside edge. *P2, k2; rep from * to last st, k1. Complete as for right front.

COLLAR

On RS, pick up and knit 82 (86, 86, 90, 90, 94) sts around collar. Work one row in k2, p2 rib.

On next row (RS), work 14 sts as set, p2tog, work 10 sts, p2tog, work 26 (30, 30, 34, 34, 38) sts, p2tog, work 10 sts, then p2tog, work 14 sts. Work one row in rib (no dec)—78 (82, 82, 86, 86, 90) sts.

NEXT ROW: Work 14 sts, k2tog, work 9, k2tog, work 24 (28, 28, 32, 32, 36), ssk, work 9, ssk, work 14. Work 3 rows as set in rib—74 (78, 78, 82, 82, 86) sts.

NEXT ROW (RS): Work 13 sts, k2tog, work 8, k2tog, work 24 (28, 28, 32, 32, 36), ssk, work 8, ssk, work 13. Work 3 rows even—70 (74, 74, 78, 78, 82) sts.

NEXT ROW (RS): Work 12 sts, k2tog, work 42 (46, 46, 50, 50, 54) sts, ssk, work 12 sts—68 (72, 72, 76, 76, 80) sts.

Work 10 (11, 11, 12, 12, 13) more rows in rib as set (no dec). BO all sts.

FINISHING

Using a steam iron and press cloth, block collar ribbing lightly to even sts.

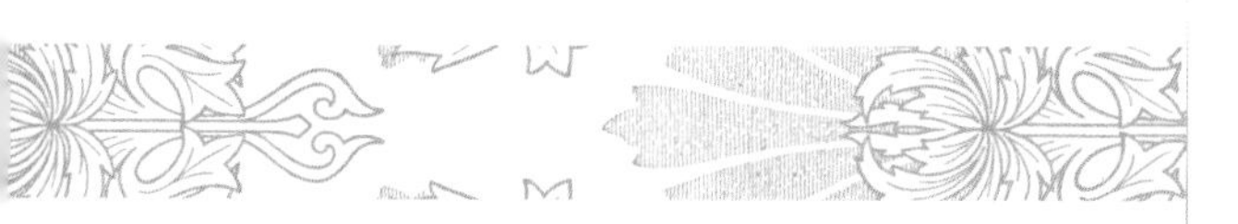

sněží OVERSIZED SHRUG

sarah shepherd

SIZES

S (M, L)

30 (32, 35½)"

Shown in size M

FINISHED MEASUREMENTS

unstretched

LENGTH (NAPE TO HEM): 27½ (28, 28½)"

WIDTH OF SHRUG (INCLUDING ARMSPAN): 53½ (54, 56)"

YARN

Debbie Bliss Pure Cashmere (100% cashmere; 49 yards/25g): 16 (16, 17) skeins, duck egg (04)

NEEDLES

5.5mm circular needles, 24" long

7.0mm circular needles, 24" long

GAUGE

13 sts and 20 rows = 4" in St st on larger needles

Sněží (pronounced snyejee) translates to "it is snowing" in Czech. It's knit on oversized needles to create a slouchy, relaxed-looking knit. A loose drape coupled with the cashmere yarn makes it the perfect wintery wrap.

pattern notes

Use long-tail method for the cast-on and an Elizabeth Zimmerman sewn bind-off (see page 84) for the cast off. This creates cast-on and bound-off edges that look the same.

Sarah is a textile designer, working primarily in feature films. She designs and creates embroideries, prints, and colors for costumes. Originally from New Zealand, she has worked there on major films such as The Lord of the Rings *and* The Last Samurai. *More recently she was chief textile artist for* The Lion, the Witch and the Wardrobe *and* Alexander. *Visit her Web site, www.sarahshepherd.com.*

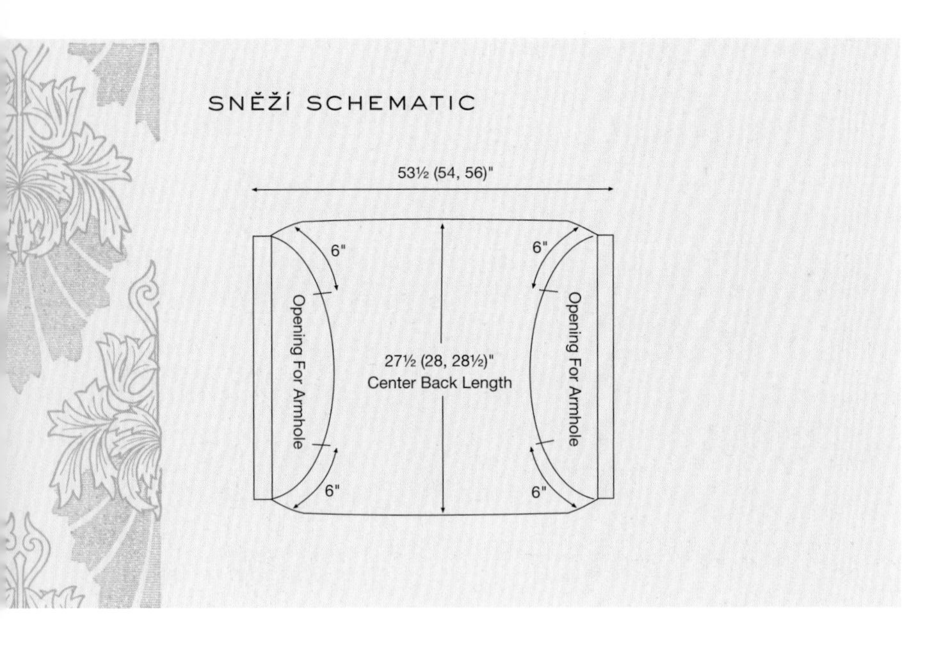

STITCH PATTERN

SEED STITCH

(over even number of sts)

ROW 1: *K1, p1; rep from * to end.

ROW 2: *P1, k1; rep from * to end.

WRAP

Using a long-tail cast-on and 5.5mm needles, CO 136 (140, 146) sts.

Work in Seed st for 10 rows. Change to 7mm needles.

ROW 11 (RS): K60 (62, 65), k1fb, *k4, k1fb rep from * three times, knit to end.

ROW 12 AND ALL WS ROWS UP TO AND INCLUDING ROW 28: Purl.

ROW 13: K62 (64, 67), k1fb, k5, k1fb, k7, k1fb, k5, k1fb, knit to end.

ROW 15: K64 (66, 69), k1fb, k6, k1fb, k5, incr1, k6, k1fb, knit to end.

ROW 17: K66 (68, 71), k1fb, k7, k1fb, k3, k1fb, k7, k1fb, knit to end.

ROW 19: K68 (70, 73) k1fb, k8, k1fb, K1, k1fb, K8, k1fb, knit to end.

ROW 21: K70 (72, 75) k1fb, k17, k1fb, knit to end.

ROW 23: K72 (74, 77) k1fb, k15, k1fb, knit to end.

ROW 25: K74 (76, 79) k1fb, k13, k1fb, knit to end.

ROW 27: K76 (78, 81) k1fb, k11, k1fb, knit to end.

ROW 29: K1, p1, k76 (78, 81), k1fb, k9, k1fb, knit to last 2 sts, p1, k1.

ROW 30 AND FOLL WS ROWS: P1, k1, purl to last 2 sts, k1, p1.

ROW 31: K1, p1, k78 (80, 82), k1fb, k7, k1fb, knit to last 2 sts, p1, k1.

ROW 33: K1, p1, k80 (82, 84), k1fb, k5, k1fb, knit to last 2 sts, p1, k1.

ROW 35: K1, p1, k82 (84, 86), k1fb, k3, k1fb, K82 knit to last 2 sts, p1, k1.

ROW 37: K1, p1, K84 (86, 88), k1fb, K1, k1fb, knit to last 2 sts, p1, k1.

For Row 39 and all RS rows until work measures 21½ (22, 22½)" from cast-on edge: K1, p1, k170 (174, 178), p1, k1.

Work even in St st for 16 rows, end with WS row.

NEXT ROW: K43 (45, 48), * sl 1, k1, psso, k2; rep from * 10 more times, **k2tog, rep from ** 10 more times, k43 (45, 48)—152 (156, 162) sts rem.

Purl 1 row.

NEXT ROW: K36 (38, 41), *sl 1, k1, psso; rep from * 19 more times, **k2tog, rep from ** 19 more times, k36 (38, 41)—112 (116, 122) sts rem.

Work even in Seed st for 10 rows.

BO using a sewn bind-off: Cut yarn leaving 3–4 times the length needed and thread through tapestry needle. Pull the needle through first two stitches as if to purl, then back through the first stitch as if to knit. Drop the first stitch off. Rep to the end.

FINISHING

Fold shrug in half so Seed st rows are on top of each other. Sew side seams together beg at cast-on/bind-off edges and cont along plain St st edges for 6" (all sizes). The unsewn sections of the side edges form armholes.

militia COAT

rain o'brien

Militia takes a period-feel military coat with a traditionally masculine style and adds sharp tailoring to make it more fitted and flattering for the feminine form. The wonderful drape of the yarn is maximized by working the body in one piece with a textured Seed stitch panel that fastens onto the front. The silk content gives a subtle sheen that adds a touch of elegance.

SIZES

XS (S, M, L, XL)

30–32 (34–36, 38–40, 42–44, 46–48)"

Shown in size S

FINISHED MEASUREMENTS

unstretched

CHEST: 34 (38, 42, 46, 50)"

LENGTH: 31½ (33, 34, 34, 35)"

SLEEVE LENGTH TO UNDERARM: 17½ (18, 18¼, 18¼, 18½)"

YARN

Sublime Cashmere Merino Silk Aran (75% extra fine merino, 20% cashmere, 5% silk; 94 yards/50g): 16 (17, 19, 21, 23) skeins, Clipper (15)

NEEDLES

5mm straight needles

NOTIONS

Twenty-six ¾" shank buttons

Two 10mm jump rings

Stitch holders or scrap yarn

GAUGE

18 sts and 24 rows = 4" in St st

pattern notes

TK2TOG: sl 1 knitwise, sl 1 tbl, transfer each st back to left needle individually and k2tog

Rain's knitting obsession (and her stash) started growing from the age of nine. Knitting plays a huge role in her life despite taking time to study for a degree in modern European languages and serve in the military. She now lives in the northwest of England and teaches languages between rows.

STITCH PATTERN

SEED STITCH

(multiple of 2 sts, 2-row repeat)

ROW 1: *K1, p1; rep from * to end.

ROW 2: *P1, k1; rep from * to end.

Repeat Rows 1 and 2.

BODY

SKIRT

Cast on 186 (198, 212, 226, 238) sts.

Work 8 rows in Seed st.

Beg working 6 (6, 8, 8, 10) rows in St st, maintaining first and last 5 sts in Seed st throughout.

DEC ROW (RS): K26 (27, 29, 30, 31), k2tog, pm, k30 (33, 36, 40, 43), pm, ssk, k56 (60, 64, 68, 72), pm, k2tog, k30 (33, 36, 40, 43), ssk, pm, k26 (27, 29, 30, 31).

Work 5 rows in St st, maintaining Seed st borders.

Rep Dec Row every 6 rows 10 more times as foll: *Work to 2 sts before marker, k2tog, sm, knit to next marker, sm, ssk; rep once from *, work to end—142 (154, 168, 182, 194) sts.

Work even for 3 (3, 5, 5, 5) rows.

WAIST SHAPING

ROW 1 (RS): * Work to 2 sts before marker, Tk2tog, sm, knit to next marker, sm, ssk; rep once from *, work to end.

ROW 2 (WS): Purl across, purling all sts decreased on previous row, tbl.

ROW 3: * Work to 1 st before marker, k1tbl, sm, knit to next marker, sm, ktbl; rep once from *, work to end.

ROW 4: Work as for Row 2.

Rep last 4 rows 2 more times, then Rows 1 and 2 only 2 (2, 2, 2, 1) time(s), then Rows 3 and 4—0 (0, 0, 0, 1) time(s).

Rep Rows 1 and 2 another 6 (6, 5, 5, 5) times, then Rows 3 and 4 another 1 (3, 5, 5, 6) time(s)—98 (110, 128, 142, 158) sts rem.

INCREASE SECTION

ROW 1 (RS): K4 (5, 8, 9, 11), M1R, k1, k1tbl, k30 (33, 36, 40, 43), k1tbl, k1, M1L, k12 (16, 22, 26, 32), M1R, k1, k1tbl, k30 (33, 36, 40, 43), k1tbl, k1, M1L, k4 (5, 8, 9, 11).

ROW 2 (WS): P6 (7, 10, 11, 13), p1tbl, p30 (33, 36, 40, 43), p1tbl, p16 (20, 26, 30, 36), p1tbl, p30 (33, 36, 40, 43), p1tbl, p6 (7, 10, 11, 13).

ROW 3: K5 (6, 9, 10, 12), M1R, k1, k1tbl, k30 (33, 36, 49, 43), k1tbl, k16 (20, 26, 30, 36), k1tbl, k30 (33, 36, 49, 43), k1tbl, k1, M1L, k5 (6, 9, 10, 12).

ROW 4: P7 (8, 11, 12, 14), p1tbl, p30 (33, 36, 49, 43), p1tbl, p16 (20, 26, 30, 36), p1tbl, p30 (33, 36, 49, 43), p1tbl, sm, p7 (8, 11, 12, 14).

Rep as for Rows 1–4, increasing as set and working previously increased sts tbl on WS rows, 3 (3, 3, 2, 2) times more.

SIZES XS (S, M) ONLY

ROW 17: K12 (13, 16), M1R, k1, k1tbl, k30 (33, 36), k1tbl, k1, M1L, k20 (24, 30), M1R, k1, k1tbl, k30 (33, 36), k1tbl, k1. M1L, k12 (13, 16).

ROW 18: P45 (49, 55), p1tbl, p24 (28, 34) p1tbl, p45 (49, 55).

ROW 19: K45 (49, 55) k1tbl, k24 (28, 34), k1tbl, k45 (49, 55).

ROW 20: As Row 18.

ROW 21: K45 (49, 55), k1tbl, k1, M1L, k22 (26, 32), M1R, k1, k1tbl, k45 (49, 55).

MILITIA SCHEMATICS

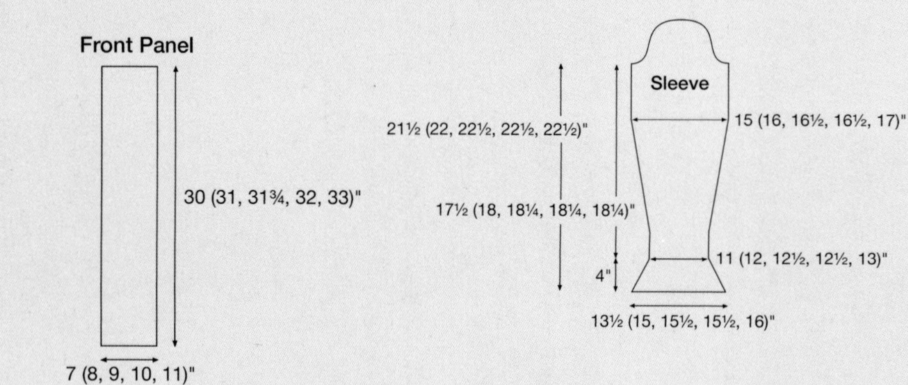

SIZE L ONLY

ROW 13: K15, M1R, k1, k1tbl, k40, k1tbl, k1, M1L, k18 32, M1R, k1, k1tbl, k40, k1tbl, k1, M1L, k15.

ROW 14: P17, p1tbl, p40, p1tbl, p36, p1tbl, k40, p1tbl, p17.

ROW 15: K16, M1R, k1, k1tbl, k40, k1tbl, k36, k1tbl, k40, k1tbl, k1, M1L, k16.

ROW 16: P59, p1tbl, p36, p1tbl, p59.

ROW 17: K59, k1tbl, k36, k1tbl, k59.

ROW 18: As Row 16.

ROW 19: K59, k1tbl, k1, M1L, k34, M1R, k1, k1tbl, k59.

ROW 20: P59, p1tbl, p38, p1tbl, p59.

ROW 21: K59, k1tbl, k38, k1tbl, k59.

SIZE XL ONLY

ROW 13: K18, k1tbl, k43, k1tbl, k1, M1L, k38, M1R, k1, k1tbl, k43, k1tbl, k18.

ROW 14: P18, p1tbl, p43, p1tbl, 42, p1tbl, k43, p1tbl, p18.

ROW 15: K17, M1R, k1, k1tbl, k43, k1tbl, k42, k1tbl, k43, k1tbl, k1, M1L, k17.

ROW 16: P63, p1tbl, p42, p1tbl, p63.

ROW 17: K63, k1tbl, k42, k1tbl, k63.

ROW 18: As Row 16.

ROW 19: K63, k1tbl, k1, M1L, k40, M1R, k1, k1tbl, k63.

ROW 20: P63, p1tbl, p44, p1tbl, p63.

ROW 21: K63, k1tbl, k44, k1tbl, k63.

ALL SIZES

ROW 22: P45 (49, 55, 59, 63), p1tbl, p26 (30, 36, 38, 44), p1tbl, p45 (49, 55, 59, 63).

ROW 23: K45 (49, 55, 59, 63), k1tbl, k26 (30, 36, 38, 44), k1tbl, k45 (49, 55, 59, 63).

ROW 24: As Row 22.

ROW 25: K45 (49, 55, 59, 63), k1tbl, k1, M1L, k24 (28, 34, 36, 42), M1R, k1, k1tbl, k45 (49, 55, 59, 63).

ROW 26: P45 (49, 55, 59, 63), p1tbl, p28 (32, 38, 40, 46), p1tbl, p45 (49, 55, 59, 63).

ROW 27: K45 (49, 55, 59, 63), k1tbl, k28 (32, 38, 40, 46), k1tbl, k45 (49, 55, 59, 63).

Rep last 2 rows twice more and then row 26 again.

ROW 33: K45 (49, 55, 59, 63), k1tbl, k1, M1L, k26 (30, 36, 38, 44), M1R, k1, k1tbl, k45 (49, 55, 59, 63).

ROW 34: P45 (49, 55, 59, 63), p1tbl, p30 (34, 40, 42, 48), p1tbl, p45 (49, 55, 59, 63).

ROW 35: K45 (49, 55, 59, 63), k1tbl, k30 (34, 40, 42, 48), k1tbl, k45 (49, 55, 59, 63).

Rep last 2 rows twice more and then Row 34 once.

SIZES XS (S, M, L) ONLY

ROW 41: K45 (49, 55, 59, 63), k1tbl, k1, M1L, k28 (32, 38, 40, 46), M1R, k1, k1tbl, k45 (49, 55, 59, 63).

SIZE XL ONLY

ROW 41: K63, k1tbl, k48, k1tbl, k63—134 (146, 164, 174, 186) sts.

DIVIDE FOR ARMHOLES

Maintaining 5-st Seed st border at either end, p20 (22, 26, 27, 29), BO 6 (6, 6, 6, 6), p72 (80, 90, 98, 106), BO 6 (6, 6, 6, 6), p20 (22, 26, 27, 29).

Turn and work on Seed st border plus first 20 (22, 25, 26, 28) sts, placing rem sts on holder.

RIGHT FRONT

Work to last 5 sts, k2tog, k3.

Purl 1 row.

Rep these 2 rows 3 (3, 4, 4, 4) times more.

Work even as set until piece measures 5½ (6, 6, 6, 6)" from beg of armhole shaping, ending with RS row

Work Seed st border and leave these 5 sts on holder, *purl to end.

K2, ssk, k to end.

Rep from * 3 times more—12 (14, 16, 18, 20) sts.

Work even for 3 (3, 5, 5, 5) rows.

SHAPE SHOULDER

BO 6 (7, 8, 9, 10) sts at beg of next and foll alt row.

LEFT FRONT

Complete as for right front, reversing all shaping and substituting k2tog for ssk.

BACK

Place rem 72 (80, 90, 98, 106) sts on needles with RS facing.

K3, ssk, k to last 5 sts, k2tog, k3.

Purl 1 row

Rep last 2 rows 3 (3, 4, 4, 4) times more.

Work even in St st until the same number of rows have been worked as for right front to start of shoulder shaping.

BO 6 (7, 8, 9, 10) sts at beg of next 4 rows.

BO rem 40 (44, 48, 52, 56) sts.

FRONT PANEL

CO 32 (36, 40, 45, 50) sts.

Work 2 (4, 4, 4, 4) rows in Seed st.

Maintaining st patt, work buttonholes over next 2 rows as foll:

ROW 1: Work 3 sts, BO 2 sts, work to last 5 sts, BO 2 sts.

ROW 2: Work 3 sts, CO 2 sts, work to last 3 sts, CO 2 sts.

*Work 20 (20, 21, 21, 21) rows in Seed st.

Work Rows 1 and 2.

Rep from * 7 times more.

Work 2 (4, 4, 4, 4) rows in Seed st.

BO in Seed st.

SLEEVES (MAKE 2)

Cast on 64 (68, 70, 70, 72) sts.

Work 4 rows in Seed st.

Work 3 sts, BO 2 sts, work to last 5 sts, BO 2 sts, work to end.

Work 3 sts, CO 2 sts, work to last 3 sts, CO 2 sts, work to end.

Maintaining st patt, dec 1 st each end next and every foll 3rd row 6 times—50 (54, 56, 56, 58) sts.

Work 3 rows in Seed st.

Change to St st and work 24 rows even.

Inc 1 st each end next and every foll 6th row 8 times as foll:

K3, M1L, work to last 3 sts, M1R, k3—68 (72, 74, 74, 76) sts. Work even until sleeve measures 21½ (22, 22½, 22½, 22½)" or desired length from CO edge.

BO 3 sts at beg of next 2 rows

K3, ssk, work to last 5 sts, k2tog, k3.

Purl 1 row.

Rep these last 2 rows 3 (3, 4, 4, 4) times more.

BO 3 sts at beg every row until 9 (10, 10, 10, 9) sts rem.

BO rem sts and fasten off.

BELT

CO 27 (31, 35, 39, 45) sts.

Work 1 row in Seed st.

Maintaining st patt, inc 1 st each end next row and EOR 4 times.

Work 4 sts, BO 2 sts, work to last 6 sts, BO 2 sts, work to end.

Work 4 sts, CO 2 sts, work to last 4 sts, CO 2 sts, work to end.

Maintaining st patt, dec 1 st each end next row and EOR 4 times.

Work 1 row.

BO in patt.

FINISHING

Block main piece to measurements in schematic. Join shoulder seams.

COLLAR

With RS facing, work 5 Seed sts from holder, pick up 12 (14, 16, 16, 18) sts along right neck shaping, 40 (44, 48, 52, 56) sts from back, 11 (13, 15, 15, 17) sts from left neck shaping, work 5 Seed sts from second holder—73 (81, 89, 93, 101) sts.

Work 5 rows in Seed st.

Maintaining st patt, dec 6 sts on next row and every 6th row to 49 (57, 65, 69, 77) sts as foll:

Work 16 (18, 20, 21, 23) sts, work 3 tog, work 16 (18, 20, 21, 23) sts, work 3 tog, work 16 (18, 20, 21, 23) sts, work 3 tog, work 16 (18, 20, 21, 23) sts.

Work 15 (17, 19, 20, 22) sts, work 3 tog, work 14 (16, 18, 19, 21) sts, work 3 tog, work 14 (16, 18, 19, 21) sts, work 3 tog, work 15 (17, 19, 20, 22) sts.

Work 14 (16, 18, 19, 21) sts, work 3 tog, work 12 (14, 16, 17, 19) sts, work 3 tog, work 12 (14, 16, 17, 19) sts, work 3 tog, work 14 (16, 18, 19, 21) sts.

Work 13 (15, 17, 18, 20) sts, work 3 tog, work 10 (12, 14, 15, 17) sts, work 3 tog, work 10 (12, 14, 15, 17) sts, work 3 tog, work 13 (15, 17, 18, 20) sts—49 (57, 65, 69, 77) sts.

Work 18 more rows, increasing 1 st each end next and EOR.

Continuing incs as set, work buttonholes as foll:

Work 3 sts, BO 2 sts, work to last 5 sts, BO 2 sts, work to end.

Work 3 sts, CO 2 sts, work to last 3 sts, CO 2 sts, work to end.

Work 4 more rows—73 (81, 89, 93, 101) sts.

BO in Seed st.

Block collar. Block front panel to match length of Seed st border on main piece.

Block belt.

Seam the sleeves and sew them to the body.

Sew buttons to Seed st borders and neck to opposite buttonholes of front panel and collar. Sew buttons to back so belt fits across small of the back. Make 2 cufflinks to be used for holding cuffs when turned back by attaching 2 shank buttons back-to-back with jump rings.

balloon sleeve JACKET

olga buraya-kefelian

This updated version of a vintage jacket is complemented by a high-fashion design—voluminous, balloon-like sleeves and an oversized collar. The close-fitting belted silhouette offers a very feminine and flattering fit. Like many classic garments, this jacket will always stay in style. Accessorize this cashmere and silk blend with luxury!

SIZES

XS (S, M, L, XL, 2X)

30 (32, 36, 40, 44, 48)"

Shown in size S

FINISHED MEASUREMENTS

CHEST (CLOSED): 31 (33, 37, 41, 45, 49)"

LENGTH: (22, 22½, 23, 23½, 24)"

UPPER ARM CIRCUMFERENCE: 9¼ (10½, 11¾, 12¼, 14¼, 15½)"

SLEEVE LENGTH: 17½ (18, 18½, 19, 19½, 20)"

YARN

Elsebeth Lavold Silky Cashmere (55% silk, 45% cashmere; 44 yards/25g): 22 (23, 26, 29, 32, 35) skeins, Wine (#005)

NEEDLES

4mm straight needles

5mm straight needles

4mm dpns

NOTIONS

Six 1¼" shank buttons

One 2½" round plastic belt buckle

Seven clothes snaps

Stitch holders

Stitch markers

Several yards scrap

GAUGE

16 sts and 25 rows = 4" in stitch patt

pattern notes

All collar shaping is done on WS.

Olga has been knitting since the age of four and has been creating her own garments for the past nine years. She enjoys the challenge that each garment brings and acquires her inspiration from current runway trends. She lives with her husband and crazy cat in Alexandria, Virginia. You can see more of her everyday knitwear adventures at www.olgajazzy.com.

SPECIAL STITCHES

KRL: insert RH needle into right leg of stitch just below next stitch; place it onto LH needle and knit it; then knit the stitch on needle

KLL: insert LH needle into left leg of stitch two rows below last completed stitch; nit this stitch through the back loop

STITCH PATTERN

(Multiple of 2 sts; 4 row repeat)

ROW 1 (RS): *K1, p1; rep from * across.

ROW 2: *K1, p1; rep from * across.

ROW 3: *P1, k1; rep from * across.

ROW 4: *P1, k1; rep from * across.

BACK

HEM

Using provisional cast-on and 5mm needles, CO 62 (66, 74, 82, 90, 98) sts. Work 7 rows in St st, ending with RS row. Knit next row for hem turning ridge.

BODY

Work even in patt st for 2¼ (2½, 2¾, 3, 3¼, 3½)".

WAIST SHAPING

DEC ROW (RS): *K2tog, work to last 2 sts, ssk. Work even for 5 rows.

Rep from * 3 more times—54 (58, 66, 74, 82, 90) sts rem.

Work even for 2½ (2¾, 3, 3¼, 3½, 3¾)".

INC ROW (RS): *K1, KLL, work to last 2 sts, KRL, K1. Work even for 5 (5, 5, 6, 6, 6) rows.

Rep from * 4 more times—64 (68, 76, 84, 92, 100) sts.

Work even until back measures 13½ (14, 14½, 15, 15½, 16)" from hem turning ridge.

ARMHOLE SHAPING

BO 2 (2, 3, 4, 5, 7) sts at beg of next 2 rows.

BO 1 (1, 2, 2, 3, 3) sts at beg of next 2 rows.

BO 0 (1, 1, 1, 2, 3) st at beg of next 2 rows.

BO 0 (0, 0, 1, 1, 1) st at beg of next 2 rows—58 (60, 64, 68, 70, 72) sts rem.

Work even until armhole measures 5 (5½, 6, 6½, 7, 7½)".

NECK SHAPING

NEXT ROW (RS): Work 22 (23, 24, 26, 27, 27) sts, BO 14 (14, 16, 16, 16, 18) sts, work to end of row.

Place first 22 (23, 24, 26, 27, 27) sts (right shoulder) on stitch holder.

LEFT SHOULDER DECREASE

NEXT ROW (WS): *Work to last 2 sts, p2tog. Work even for 1 row.

Rep from * 3 more times—18 (19, 20, 22, 23, 23) sts rem. (WS) BO 4 (4, 5, 6, 7, 8) sts at beg of row—11(12, 14, 16, 18, 20) sts rem.

Work even for 1 row.

(WS) BO 4 (4, 5, 6, 7, 8) sts at beg of row.

(RS) BO rem 7 (8, 9, 10, 11, 12) sts.

CONTINUE NECK SHAPING AND RIGHT SHOULDER DECREASE

Sl sts from st holder back to needle

Work WS row in patt. On RS row, work to last 2 sts, k2tog.

Complete shaping as for left shoulder, substituting k2tog for all p2tog decs.

LEFT FRONT

HEM

Using provisional cast-on and 5mm needles, CO 38 (42, 50, 58, 66, 74) sts. Work 7 rows in St st ending with a RS row. Knit next row for hem turning ridge.

BODY

Beg st patt and work 8 rows ending with RS row. CO 4 sts for self-facing using backward loop cast-on—42 (46, 54, 62, 70, 78) sts.

Working 4 newly cast-on sts in St st, continue body in patt st until piece measures 2¼ (2½, 2¾, 3, 3¼, 3½)" from hem turning ridge.

WAIST SHAPING

DEC ROW (RS): *K2tog, work in patt to end of row. Work even for 5 rows.

Rep from * 3 more times—38 (42, 50, 58, 66, 74) sts rem.

Work even for 2½ (2¾, 3, 3¼, 3½, 3¾)".

INC ROW (RS): *K1, KLL, work in patt to end of row. Work even for 5 rows.

Rep from * 4 more times—43 (47, 55, 63, 71, 79) sts rem.

Work even until front measures 13½ (14, 14½, 15, 15½, 16)" from hem turning ridge.

ARMHOLE SHAPING

Continue in st patt, shaping armhole as follows:

DEC ROW 1: BO 2 (2, 3, 4, 5, 7) sts at beg of row.

DEC ROW 2: BO 1 (1, 2, 2, 3, 3) sts at beg of row.

DEC ROW 3: BO 0 (1, 1, 1, 2, 3) st at beg of row.

DEC ROW 4: BO 0 (0, 0, 1, 1, 1) st at beg of row—40 (43, 49, 55, 60, 65) sts rem.

Work even until armhole measures 4 (4½, 5, 5½, 6, 6½)".

NECKLINE SHAPING

NEXT ROW (WS): Place 4 sts of self-facing and 12 (14, 19, 23, 27, 32) sts of body on st holder, BO 5 sts, work to end—23 (24, 25, 27, 28, 28) sts rem.

NEXT ROW (RS): *Work to last 2 sts, ssk.

Work even for 1 row.

Rep from * until 18 (19, 20, 22, 23, 23) sts rem.

Beg shoulder decs:

(RS) BO 5 (5, 5, 6, 6, 6) sts, work to last 2 sts, ssk.

NEXT ROW: BO 4 (4, 5, 5, 5, 5) sts, work to end.

BO rem 8 (9, 9, 10, 11, 11) sts.

RIGHT FRONT

Work as for left front, reversing shaping and substituting k2tog for ssk.

SLEEVES (MAKE 2)

Using provisional cast-on and 4mm dpns, CO 25 (30, 35, 35, 35, 40) sts. Join for working in the rnd, being careful not to twist, and pm to indicate beg of rnd. Work 6 rnds in St st. Purl 1 rnd, knit 6 more rnds. Place sts from provisional cast-on on a separate needle. On next rnd, align CO row with current row and form sleeve hem by knitting each "live" st tog with matching st from cast-on edge.

Purl 2 rnds.

BALLOON

SET-UP RND: *P2 (3, 2, 2, 2, 4), pm, p3 (3, 3, 3, 3, 4) pm; rep from * around.

Work balloon increases:

NEXT (INC) RND: *P1fb, p0 (1, 0, 0, 0, 2), p1bf, sm, p3, sm; rep from * around—35 (40, 45, 45, 45, 50) sts.

Purl 2 rnds.

NEXT (INC) RND: *P1fb, purl to 1 st before marker, p1bf, sm, purl to next marker, sm; rep from * around—45 (50, 55, 55, 55, 60) sts.

Rep last 3 rnds twice more—65 (70, 75, 75, 75, 80) sts.

Do not remove st markers

Purl 12 rnds.

WORK DECREASES

NEXT (DEC) RND: *P2tog, purl to 2 sts before marker, ssp, sm, purl to next marker, sm; rep from * around—55 (60, 65, 65, 65, 70) sts rem.

Purl 2 rnds.

Rep last 3 rnds 3 (3, 3, 3, 2, 2) times more, removing all markers on last dec rnd—25 (30, 35, 35, 45, 50) sts rem.

NOTE: Sleeve is worked flat from this point on.

INC ROW: *K1, KLL, work in st patt to last 2 sts, KRL, k1. Work 5 (5, 6, 6, 7, 7) rows even. Rep from * 8 times—41 (46, 51, 53, 61, 66) sts.

ARMHOLE SHAPING

BO 2 (2, 3, 4, 5, 7) sts at beg of next 2 rows.

BO 1 (1, 2, 1, 1, 1) st(s) at beg of next 2 rows.

BO 0 (1, 1, 1, 1, 1) st at beg of next 2 rows—35 (38, 39, 41, 47, 48) sts rem.

Work even for 2 (2½, 3, 3½, 4, 4½)".

BO 2 sts at beg of next two rows—31 (34, 35, 37, 43, 44) sts rem.

Work 2 rows even.

BO 1 st at beg of next 4 rows.

BO 2 sts at beg of next 2 rows.

BO 2 sts at beg of next 2 rows.

BO 3 sts at beg of next 2 rows.

BO 4 sts beg of next 2 rows.

BO rem 9 (12, 13, 15, 21, 22) sts.

COLLAR

Using long-tail cast-on and 4mm needles, CO 16 (17, 17, 17, 18, 18) sts.

(WS) *Work to end of row. Add 1 st using backward loop cast-on.

Work even for 1 row.

Rep from * 2 more times—19 (20, 20, 20, 21, 21) sts.

(WS) *SSK, work to end, backward loop cast-on 1 st.

Work even for 1 row.

Rep from * 3 more times.

Work even for 4 rows.

SHORT-ROWING

ROW 1 (RS): Work 17 (18, 18, 18, 19, 19) sts, sl 1 st, wrap yarn from back to front, sl st back to left needle. Turn work to WS.

BALLOON SLEEVE JACKET SCHEMATICS

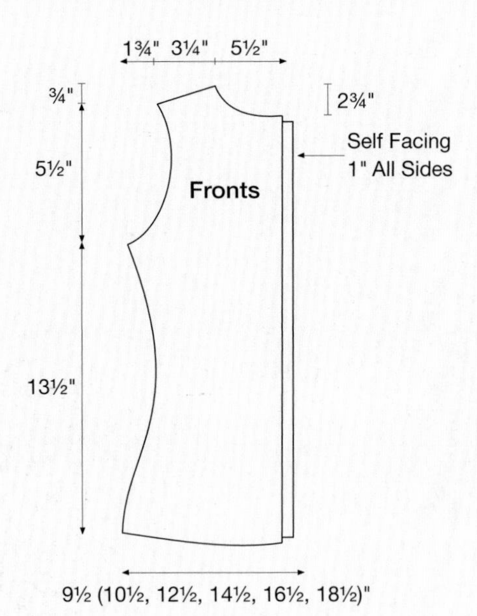

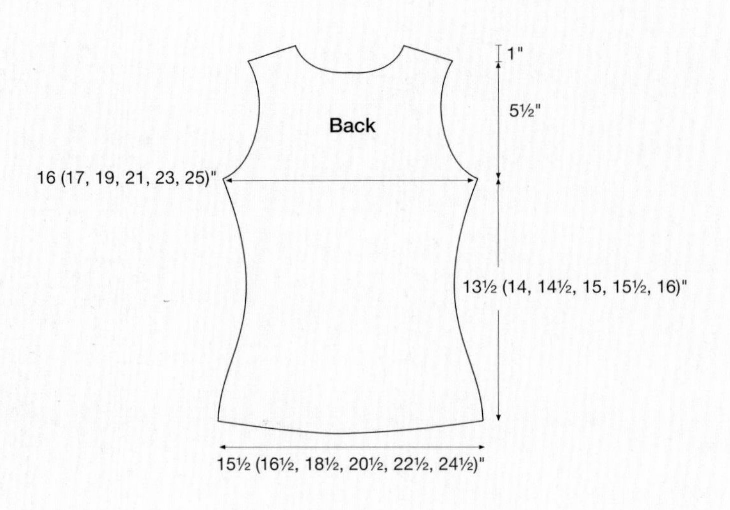

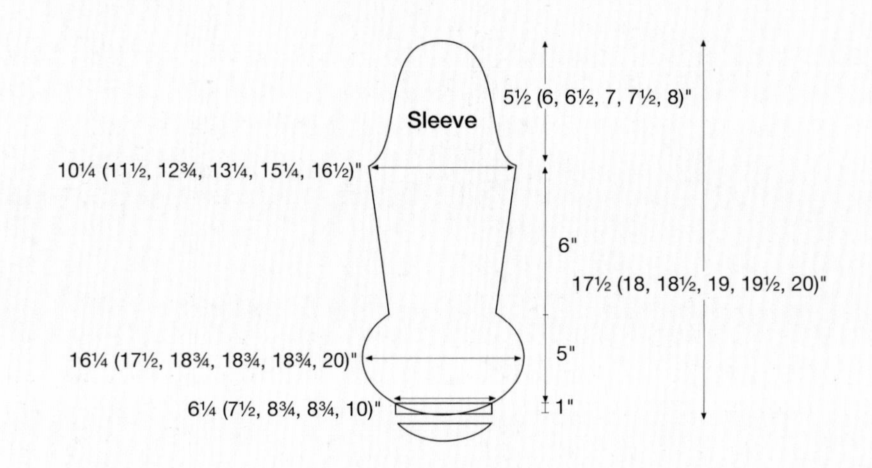

ROW 2: Work to end of row.

ROW 3: Work row to wrap, pick up wrap and st and knit them tog, knit last st.

ROW 4: Work in patt.

Rep Rows 1–4 until work at mid-row measures 19 (20, 20, 21, 21, 22)" from beg of short-rows.

Work even for 4 rows.

(WS) K1fb in first st, work to last 2 sts, k2tog.

Continue in this manner EOR 3 more times.

(WS) Work row to last 2 sts, k2tog.

Rep EOR 2 more times.

BO rem 16 (17, 17, 17, 18, 18) sts.

BELT

Using long-tail cast-on method and 4mm needles, CO 11 sts. Adjust number of patt sts to accommodate a larger or smaller belt buckle.

Work in st patt until belt measures 34 (36, 40, 44, 48, 52)".

TIP SHAPING

ROW 1: K2tog, work 7, ssk—9 sts rem.

ROWS 2 AND 4: Work even in patt.

ROW 3: K2tog, work 5, ssk—7 sts rem.

BO rem 7 sts.

Secure and weave in ends.

FINISHING

Steam pieces of jacket. Sleeves should be stuffed with cloth or towels prior to steaming to preserve their shape. Allow pieces to cool.

Steam bottom and side hems at edges for easier seaming. Whipstitch sts from provisionally cast-on hem edge to inside of jacket body. Sew self-facing hems to inside of jacket fronts. Using Kitchener st (see Special Techniques, page 137), sew the live sts from stitch holders to inside of jacket fronts.

Sew shoulder and side seams; set in sleeves.

Attach buckle to belt.

Pin or baste collar to neck edge, gently stretching edges to fit, and sew.

Sew in snaps and buttons as shown.

CHAPTER FOUR

FEMININE MYSTIQUE

dresses to capture their attention

jewel MINI DRESS

anna bell

Sometimes you have to let the yarn do the work to create this kind of glamour. This beautiful cobalt blue silk-cashmere blend is wonderfully soft next to the skin. The short dress/tunic fastens at the back of the neck with a bow and lets the yarn take center stage. Worked in one piece, there is no finishing beyond weaving in ends.

SIZES

XS (S, M, L, XL)

32 (34, 36, 38, 40)"

Shown in size S

FINISHED MEASUREMENTS

unstretched

BUST: 38 (40, 42, 44, 46)"

LENGTH FROM UNDERARM: 25 (25, 26, 26, 27)"

YARN

Posh Yarns Eva (55% silk, 45% cashmere; 109 yards/55g): 10 (11, 12, 13, 15) skeins, Cobalt

NEEDLES

4.5mm circulars, 24" long

5mm circulars, 24" long

4.5mm dpns

NOTIONS

Stitch markers

Stitch holders

Large safety pin

Tapestry needle

Cable needles (or use dpn)

GAUGE

16 sts and 22 rows = 4" in St St

pattern notes

The shoulder straps with slipped-stitch edgings will pucker as you are working them but should block flat.

Anna lives in London, where she spends her time knitting, writing, and writing about knitting. She learned to knit as a child, has been designing since 2005, and is currently working on a collection for a book due out in 2009. You can read about Anna's adventures in yarn at her Web site: needleandhook.co.uk/journal.

DRESS

Using 5mm needles, CO 154 (162, 170, 178, 186) sts and join for working in the rnd, taking care not to twist stitches. Pm to show beg of rnd. Work 8 rnds in St st (knit every rnd).

Fold work wrong side inwards. Knit each st together with its equivalent on cast-on edge to make hem.

Cont in St st until work measures 9 (9, 9½, 9½, 10)" from fold of hem. Change to smaller needle.

CASING FOR CORD

K1fb every stitch—308 (324, 340, 354, 368) sts.

RND 1: (K1, sl 1 wyif) to end of rnd.

RND 2: (Sl 1 wyib, p1) to end of rnd.

Rep last 2 rnds.

MAKE EYELETS

RND 1: (K1, sl 1 wyif) twice. *Slip next st to RH needle. Place next st on cable needle and hold at back of work. Return slipped st on RH needle to LH needle. Slip st from cable needle to RH needle, with yarn held in front. Yarn over, ssk. Sl 1 wyif ,** (k1, sl 1 wyif) to last 6 sts. Rep from * to **, (k1, sl 1 wyif) to end of rnd.

RND 2: (Sl 1 wyib, p1) twice. P1, sl next st (yarn over from previous rnd) wyib. (sl 1 wyib, p1) to last 6 sts. P1, sl next st wyib. (Sl 1 wyib, p1) to end of rnd.

RND 3: (K1, sl 1 wyif) twice. *Slip next st to cable needle and hold at back of work. K1 (into yarn over), slip st from cable needle to RH needle, with yarn held in front. Sl 1 wyif.** (K1, sl 1 wyif) to last 6 sts. Rep from * to **. (K1, sl 1 wyif) to end of rnd.

RND 4: (Sl 1 wyib, p1) to end of rnd. Change to larger needle.

NEXT RND: Ssk across all sts—154 (162, 170, 178, 186) sts.

Cont without shaping until work measures 25 (25, 26, 26, 27)" from fold of hem.

Work 77 (81, 85, 89, 93) sts and leave on scrap yarn or spare needle for front armhole.

BACK ARMHOLE SHAPING

BO 4 (4, 5, 5, 6) sts, k17 (19, 20, 22, 23), (k2tog, k1) 12 times, k16 (18, 19, 21, 22), k4 (4, 5, 5, 6)—61 (65, 68, 72, 75) sts. Turn work.

BO 26 (30, 33, 30, 33) sts and purl to end—35 (35, 35, 42, 42) sts.

NEXT ROW (RS): Dec 1 st at beg of next row.

NEXT ROW (WS): BO 2 (2, 2, 5, 5) sts at beg of row, dec 1 st at end of row.

NEXT ROW (RS): Dec 1 st at beg of row.

NEXT ROW (WS): BO 2 (2, 2, 4, 4) sts at beg of row—28 (28, 28, 30, 30) sts.

Dec 1 st at beg of each RS row 4 (4, 4, 6, 6) times, AT THE SAME TIME, BO 2 sts at beg of each WS row 4 times—16 sts.

BO 1 st at beg of each WS row until 8 sts rem. Leave 8 sts on holder for back shoulder strap.

FRONT ARMHOLE SHAPING

Return 77 (81, 85, 89, 93) sts to working needle. With RS facing, rejoin yarn and BO 4 (4, 5, 5, 6) sts. K17 (19, 20, 22, 23), (k2tog, k1) 12 times, k16 (18, 19, 21, 22), k4 (4, 5, 5, 6)—61 (65, 68, 72, 75) sts. Turn work.

BO 4 (4, 5, 5, 6) sts and purl to end—57 (61, 63, 67, 69) sts.

NEXT ROW (RS): BO 4 (5, 5, 6, 6) sts at beg of row, dec 1 st at end of row.

NEXT ROW (WS): Dec 1 st at beg of row—51 (54, 56, 59, 61) sts.

NEXT ROW (RS): BO 4 (5, 5, 6, 6) sts at beg of row, dec 1 st at end of row. Work 1 row without shaping.

Rep last 2 rows 4 times more—26 (24, 26, 24, 26) sts.

BO 3 sts at beg of next 3 RS rows—17 (15, 17, 15, 17) sts. Dec 1 st at beg of each foll RS row 9 (7, 9, 7, 9) times—8 sts rem, ending with WS row. Leave sts on holder.

I-CORD EDGING

With RS facing and smaller circular needle, pick up and knit 55 (55, 57, 59, 59) sts around right armhole. Break yarn.

With 4.5mm dpn and scrap yarn, CO 4 sts. Break yarn. Join working yarn and knit 4 sts. Do not turn work.

*With RS facing, slide sts to right end of dpn. K3 sts, pulling first st tight. Last st, ssk with first st of armhole sts on circular needle (RS facing). Rep from * until all armhole sts have been worked to form I-cord edging. Break yarn.

With RS facing, slide sts to right end of dpn. Slip first 2 sts onto RH needle. Turn this needle 180 degrees so that first 2 sts are held at back of work and have wrong sides facing. Using 3rd needle, slip 1 st from back needle, then 1 st from front needle. Rep, adding all 4 sts to 8 sts on holder for back shoulder strap—12 sts total.

Carefully unpick provisional cast-on and place all 4 sts on dpn. With WS facing, *slip first 2 sts onto second dpn needle. Turn this needle 180 degrees so that first 2 sts are held at front of work and have right sides facing. Using 3rd needle, slip 1 st from back needle, then 1 st from front needle. Rep, adding all 4 sts to 8 sts on holder for front shoulder strap—12 sts total.

BACK ARMHOLE SHAPING

With RS facing and smaller circular needle, pick up and knit 108 (114, 118, 124, 128) sts from back shoulder strap, around left armhole, and along front edge to front shoulder strap. Break yarn. Complete I-cord edging as for front armhole—do not break yarn. With RS facing, incorporate edging into shoulder strap as above from *. K8 sts from holder, (sl 1 wyif, k1) twice—16 sts.

FRONT SHOULDER STRAP

WS: (Sl 1 wyif, k1) twice, p8, (sl 1 wyif, k1) twice.

RS: (Sl 1 wyif, k1) twice, k8, (sl 1 wyif, k1) twice.

Rep last two rows until shoulder strap measures 27" from start of armhole shaping, ending with RS row.

NEXT ROW (WS): (Sl 1 wyif, k1) twice, p1fb 8 times, (sl 1 wyif, k1) twice—24 sts.

RS: (Sl 1 wyif, k1) to end.

WS: (Sl 1 wyif, k1) to end.

Rep last 2 rows.

K2tog twice. BO 1 st by passing first st on RH needle off and over second st. Cont until all sts are bound off.

BACK SHOULDER STRAP

Work as for front shoulder strap, picking up 12 sts from holder—16 sts. Join in yarn, turn work. Complete as for front.

I-CORD

Using dpn, cast on 4 sts. Work in I-cord for 62". BO.

FINISHING

Weave in all ends. Block thoroughly. Attach large safety pin to one end of I-cord and feed it through casing, entering and exiting all eyelets.

arris BEADED DRESS

sauniell n. connally

With beading and cable detail, this sundress is all about the sharp and sparkling angles. A combination of simple stitches and cables give the look of a very complex design. The coordinating glass beads highlight the cables and give a hint of style that makes this dress perfect for day or evening. The cotton/cashmere blend also makes this a well structured, yet soft and comfortable dress.

SIZES

S (M, L, XL)

32–34 (36–38, 40–42, 44–46)"

Shown in size S

FINISHED MEASUREMENTS

unstretched

BUST: 32 (36, 40, 43)"

HIP: 37 (42, 47, 52)"

YARN

Debbie Bliss Cotton Cashmere (85% cotton, 15% cashmere; 105 yards/50g): 12 (14, 16, 17) skeins, Cream (02)

NEEDLES

3.75mm circulars, 32" long

3.75mm dpns

NOTIONS

Beads size 6/0 – 900 (1000, 1100, 1200)

Stitch markers

Stitch holder

Tapestry needle

Cable needle

Beading needle

GAUGE

23 sts and 30 rows = 4" in St st

pattern notes

Read entire pattern before beginning.

For the sake of readability, after round 35, only the beginning and ending stitches of each side of the round will be written. The core of the round will be omitted. Omitted text will be denoted as "work center sts." Cont to work center stitches and cables as set in pattern.

BEADING YARN: Rewind yarn and check for knots before stringing beads. Using a "big-eye" beading needle, string approximately 40 beads per skein.

Sauniell's designs have appeared in knit simple *and* knit 1 *as well as the web knitting magazine Magknits.com. She believes in designing fashionable yet classic items, and will not design anything she would not wear herself. Visit her blog at saunshine.blogspot.com.*

SPECIAL STITCHES

SLB (SLIP BEAD): yfwd, position 1 bead, slip 1 st, yb

HOLD: slip sts to cable needle

LT (LEFT TWIST): hold st to front, k1, k st from holder

LTPB (LEFT TWIST PURL BACK): hold st to front, p1, k st from holder

RT (RIGHT TWIST): hold st to back, k1, k st from holder

RTPB (RIGHT TWIST PURL BACK): hold st to back, k1, p st from holder

2LTPB: LTPB, slb, LTPB

2RTPB: RTPB, slb, RTPB

LLTPB: LT, slb, LTPB

RRTPB: RTPB, slb, RT

SKIRT

Using 3.75mm needles, cast on 288 (316, 344, 372) sts, pm after 144 (158, 172, 186) sts. Join for working in rnd, being careful not to twist, and pm. Knit 2 rows.

RND 1: *2LTPB, k22, LLTPB, p22, 2LTPB, k26 (40, 54, 68), 2RTPB, p22, RRTPB, k22, 2RTPB, sm, rep from *.

RND 2: *P1, k1, p2, k25, p2, k1, p23, k1, p2, k28 (42, 56, 70), p2, k1, p23, k1, p2, k25, p2, k1, p1, sm, rep from *.

From this point on, work even numbered rows as foll: knit the knit sts, purl the purl sts.

RND 3: *P1, 2LTPB, k22, LLTPB, p22, 2LTPB, k24 (38, 52, 66), 2RTPB, p22, RRTPB, k22, 2RTPB, p1, sm, rep from *.

RND 5: *P2, 2LTPB, k22, LLTPB, p22, 2LTPB, k22 (36, 50, 64), 2RTPB, p22, RRTPB, k22, 2RTPB, p2, sm, rep from *.

RND 7: *P3, 2LTPB, k22, LLTPB, p22, 2LTPB, k20 (34, 48, 62), 2RTPB, p22, RRTPB, k22, 2RTPB, p3, sm, rep from *.

RND 9: *P4, 2LTPB, k22, LLTPB, p22, 2LTPB, k18 (32, 46, 60), 2RTPB, p22, RRTPB, k22, 2RTPB, p4, sm, rep from *.

RND 11: *P2tog, p3, 2LTPB, k22, LLTPB, p22, 2LTPB, k16 (30, 44, 58), 2RTPB, p22, RRTPB, k22, 2RTPB, p3, p2tog, sm, rep from *—284 (312, 340, 368) sts.

RND 13: *P5, 2LTPB, k22, LLTPB, p22, 2LTPB, k14 (28, 42, 56), 2RTPB, p22, RRTPB, k22, 2RTPB, p5, sm, rep from *.

RND 15: *P6, 2LTPB, k22, LLTPB, p22, 2LTPB, k12 (26, 40, 54), 2RTPB, p22, RRTPB, k22, 2RTPB, p6, sm, rep from *.

RND 17: *P2tog, p5, 2LTPB, k22, LLTPB, p22, 2LTPB, k10 (24, 38, 52), 2RTPB, p22, RRTPB, k22, 2RTPB, p5, p2tog, sm, rep from *—280 (308, 336, 364) sts.

RND 19: *P7, 2LTPB, k22, LLTPB, p22, 2LTPB, k8 (22, 36, 50), 2RTPB, p22, RRTPB, k22, 2RTPB, p7, sm, rep from *.

RND 21: *P8, 2LTPB, k22, LLTPB, p22, 2LTPB, k6 (20, 34, 48), 2RTPB, p22, RRTPB, k22, 2RTPB, p8, sm, rep from *.

RND 23: *P2tog, p7, 2LTPB, k22, LLTPB, p22, 2LTPB, k4 (18, 32, 46), 2RTPB, p22, RRTPB, k22, 2RTPB, p7, p2tog, sm, rep from *—276(304, 332, 360)sts.

RND 25: *P9, 2LTPB, k22, LLTPB, p22, 2LTPB, k2 (16, 30, 44), 2RTPB, p22, RRTPB, k22, 2RTPB, p9, sm, rep from *.

RND 27: *P10, 2LTPB, k22, LLTPB, p22, 2LTPB, k0 (14, 28, 42), 2RTPB, p22, RRTPB, k22, 2RTPB, p10, sm, rep from *.

FOR SIZE S (CABLE CONVERGENCE)

RND 29: *P2tog, p9, 2LTPB, k22, LLTPB, p22, LTPB, slb, p2, slb, RTPB, p22, RRTPB, k22, 2RTPB, p9, p2tog, sm, rep from *.

RND 31: *P11, 2LTPB, k22, LLTPB, p22, LTPB, p2, RTPB, p22, RRTPB, k22, 2RTPB, p11, sm, rep from *.

RND 33: *P12, 2LTPB, k22, LLTPB, p22, LTPB, RTPB, p22, RRTPB, k22, 2RTPB, p12, sm, rep from *.

FOR ALL OTHER SIZES

Continue patt as set, working cables toward the center. As cables converge, work as for size S.

RND 29: *P2tog, p9, 2LTPB work center sts, 2RTPB, p9, p2tog, sm, rep from *.

RND 31: *P11, 2LTPB, work center sts, 2RTPB, p11, sm, rep from *.

RND 33: *P12, 2LTPB, work center sts, 2RTPB, p12, sm, rep from *.

FOR ALL SIZES

RND 35: *P2tog, p11, 2LTPB, work center sts, 2RTPB, p12, p2tog, rep from *.

RND 37: *P13, 2LTPB, work center sts, 2RTPB, p13, rep from *.

RND 39: *P14, 2LTPB, work center sts, 2RTPB, p14, rep from *.

RND 41: *P2tog, p13, 2LTPB, work center sts, 2RTPB, p13, p2tog, rep from *.

RND 43: *P15, 2LTPB, work center sts, 2RTPB, p15, rep from *.

RND 45: *P16, 2LTPB, work center sts, 2RTPB, p16, rep from *.

RND 47: *P2tog, p15, 2LTPB, work center sts, 2RTPB, p15, p2tog, rep from *.

RND 49: *P17, 2LTPB, work center sts, k22, 2RTPB, p17, rep from *.

RND 51: *P18, 2LTPB, work center sts, 2RTPB, p18, rep from *.

RND 53: *P2tog, p17, 2LTPB, work center sts, 2RTPB, p17, p2tog, rep from *

RND 55: *P19, 2LTPB, work center sts, 2RTPB, p19, rep from *.

RND 57: *P20, 2LTPB, work center sts, 2RTPB, p20, rep from *.

RND 59: *P2tog, p19, 2LTPB, work center sts, 2RTPB, p19, p2tog, rep from *.

RND 61: *P21, 2LTPB, work center sts, 2RTPB, p21, rep from *.

RND 63: *P22, 2LTPB, work center sts, 2RTPB, p22, rep from *.

RND 65: *Ssk, p21, 2LTPB, work center sts, 2RTPB, p21, p2tog, rep from *.

RND 67: *LTPB, p21, 2LTPB, work center sts, 2RTPB, p21, RTPB, rep from *.

RND 69: *P1, LTPB, p21, 2LTPB, work center sts, 2RTPB, p21, RTPB, p1, rep from *.

RND 71: *P1, slb, ssk, p21, 2LTPB, work center sts, 2RTPB, p21, RTPB, slb, rep from *.

RND 73: *P1, slb, LTPB, p21, 2LTPB, work center sts, 2RTPB, p21, RTPB, slb, p1, rep from *.

RND 75: *LLTPB, p21, 2LTPB, work center sts, 2RTPB, p21, RRTPB, rep from *.

RND 77: *K1, ssk, slb, LTPB, p21, 2LTPB, work center sts, k22, 2RTPB, p21, RTFB, slb, k2tog, k1, rep from *.

RND 79: *K1, LLTPB, p21, 2LTPB, work center sts, 2RTPB, p21, RRTPB, k1, rep from *.

RND 81: *K2, LLTPB, p21, 2LTPB, work center sts, 2RTPB, p21, RRTPB, k2, rep from *.

RND 83: *K2tog, k1, LLTPB, work center sts, RRTPB, k1, ssk , rep from *.

RND 85: *K3, LLTPB, work center sts, RRTPB, k3, rep from *.

RND 87: *K4, LLTPB, work center sts, RRTPB, k4, rep from *.

RND 89: *K2tog, k3, LLTPB, work center sts, RRTPB, k3, ssk , rep from *.

RND 91: *K5, LLTPB, work center sts, p21, RRTPB, k5, rep from *.

RND 93: *K6, LLTPB, work center sts, RRTPB, k6, rep from *.

RND 95: *K2tog, k5, LLTPB, work center sts, RRTPB, k5, ssk , rep from *.

RND 97: *K7, LLTPB, work center sts, RRTPB, k7, rep from *.

RND 99: *K8, LLTPB, work center sts, RRTPB, k8, rep from *.

RND 101: *K2tog, k7, LLTPB, work center sts, RRTPB, k7, ssk, rep from *.

RND 103: *K9, LLTPB, work center sts, RRTPB, k9, rep from *.

RND 105: *K10, LLTPB, work center sts, RRTPB, k10, rep from *.

RND 107: *K2tog, k9, LLTPB, work center sts, RRTPB, k9, ssk , rep from *.

RND 109: *K11, LLTPB, work center sts, RRTPB, k11, rep from *.

RND 111: *K12, LLTPB, work center sts, RRTPB, k12, rep from *.

RND 113: *K2tog, k11, LLTPB, work center sts, RRTPB, k11, ssk , rep from *.

RND 115: *K13, LLTPB, work center sts, RRTPB, k13, rep from *.

RND 117: *K14, LLTPB, work center sts, RRTPB, k14, rep from *.

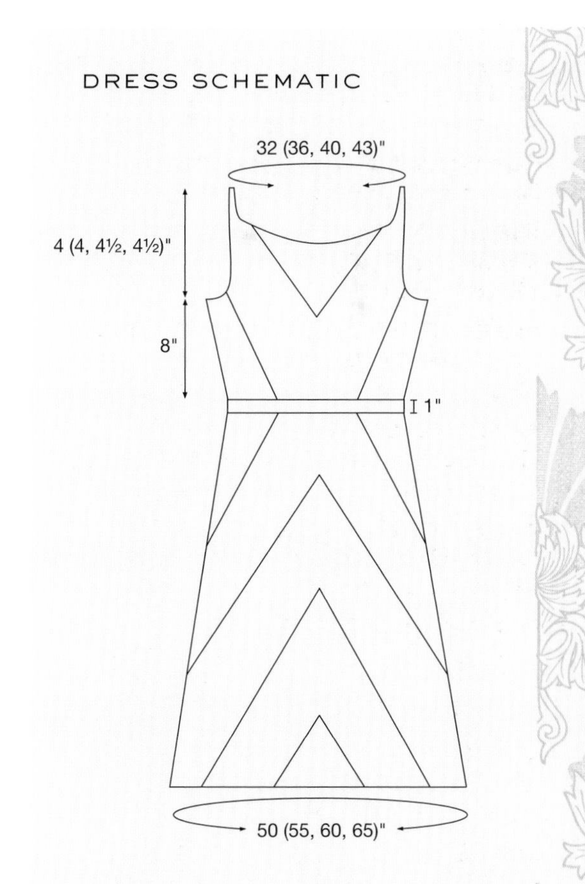

RND 119: *K2tog, k13, LLTPB, work center sts, RRTPB, k13, ssk , rep from *.

RND 121: *K15, LLTPB, work center sts, RRTPB, k15, rep from *.

RND 123: *K16, LLTPB, work center sts, RRTPB, k16, rep from *.

RND 125: *K2tog, k15, LLTPB, work center sts, RRTPB, k15, ssk, rep from *.

RND 127: *K17, LLTPB, work center sts, RRTPB, k17, rep from *.

RND 129: *K18, LLTPB, work center sts, RRTPB, k18, rep from *.

RND 131: *K2tog, k17, LLTPB, work center sts, RRTPB, k17, ssk, rep from *.

RND 133: *K19, LLTPB, work center sts, RRTPB, k19, rep from *.

RND 135: *K20, LLTPB, work center sts, RRTPB, k20, rep from *.

RND 137: *K2tog, k19, LLTPB, work center sts, RRTPB, k19, ssk, rep from *.

RND 139: *K21, LLTPB, work center sts, RRTPB, k21, rep from *.

RND 141: *K22, LLTPB, work center sts, RRTPB, k22, rep from *.

RND 143: *K2tog, k21, LLTPB, work center sts, RRTPB, k21, ssk , rep from *.

RND 145: *K23, LLTPB, work center sts, RRTPB, k23, rep from *.

RND 147: *K24, LLTPB, work center sts, RRTPB, k24, rep from *.

RND 149: *P1, ssk, k22, LLTPB, work center sts, RRTPB, k22, k2tog, p1, rep from *.

RND 151: *P1, LTPB, k22, LLTPB work center sts, RRTPB, k22, RTPB, p1, rep from *.

RND 153: *P1, slb, LTPB, k22, LLTPB, work center sts, RRTPB, k22, RTPB, slb, p1, rep from *.

RND 155: *Ssk, slb, LTPB, k22, LLTPB, work center sts, RRTPB, k22, RTPB, slb, k2tog, rep from *.

RND 157: *2LLTPB, k22, work center sts, k22, 2RRTPB, rep from *.

RND 159: *P1, 2LLTPB, work center sts, 2RRTPB, p1, rep from *.

RND 161: *P2tog, 2LLTPB, work center sts, 2RRTPB, p2tog, rep from *—184 (212, 240, 268)sts.

RND 163: *P2, 2LLTPB, work center sts, 2RRTPB, p2, rep from *.

RND 165: *P3, 2LLTPB, work center sts, 2RRTPB, p3, rep from *.

RND 167: *P4, 2LLTPB, work center sts, 2RRTPB, p4, rep from *.

RND 169: *P5, 2LLTPB, work center sts, 2RRTPB, p5, rep from *.

MIDSECTION DETAIL

RND 171: Purl all sts.

RND 173: **K5, k2tog, work [k3, k2tog] 2(2, 4, 6) times, k58 (72, 66, 60), work [k2tog, k3] 2(2, 4, 6) times, k5, and rep from ** once—172 (200, 220, 240) sts.

RND 175: Purl all sts.

RND 177: *K3, slb, and rep from * to end.

RND 179: Knit all sts.

RND 181: Purl all sts.

RND 183: Knit all sts.

RND 185: Purl all sts.

BODICE

RND 1: *P7 (7, 7, 9), RRTPB, k17 (17, 17, 20), 2RRTPB, p18 (32, 42, 42), 2LLTPB, k17 (17, 17,20), LLTPB, p7 (7, 7, 9), rep from *.

RND 3: *P6 (6, 6, 8), RRTPB, k17 (17, 17, 20), 2RRTPB, p20 (34 ,44, 44), 2LLTPB, k17 (17, 17, 20), LLTPB, p6 (6, 6, 8), rep from *.

RND 5: *Inc 1, p5 (5, 5, 7), RRTPB, k17 (17, 17, 20), 2RRTPB, p22 (36, 46, 46), 2LLTPB, k17 (17, 17, 20), LLTPB, p5 (5, 5, 7), inc 1; rep from *—176 (204, 224, 244).

Cont working in patt, working increase every 4th rnd 2 (1, 1, 1) time(s)—184 (208, 228, 248) sts.

Cont for 7 rnds.

RND 29: *Work in patt for 45 (50, 55, 60) sts, RTPB, LTPB, work 45 (50, 55, 60) sts, rep from *.

RND 31: *Work in patt for 44 (49, 54, 59) sts, RTPB, p2 LTPB, work 44 (49, 54, 59) sts, rep from *.

RND 33: *Work in patt for 43 (48, 53, 58) sts, RTPB, slb, k2, slb, LTPB, work 43 (48, 53, 58) sts, rep from *.

RND 35: *Work in patt for 42 (47, 52, 57) sts, RRTPB, LLTPB, work 42 (47, 52, 57) sts, rep from *.

RND 37: *Work in patt for 41 (46, 51, 56) sts, RRTPB, k2, LLTPB, work 41 (46, 51, 56) sts, rep from *.

Cont working in pat for 19 rnds.

NEXT RND: *Working in patt, BO 5 (5, 6, 6) sts, work 36 (40, 44, 48) sts, BO 10 (14, 14, 16) sts, work 36 (40, 44, 48) sts, BO 5 (5, 6, 6) sts, and rep from *. Break yarn.

TOP BACK

RIGHT SIDE

NEXT ROW (WS): Attach yarn at center and BO 4 sts and work to end, working sts as they lay.

NEXT ROW (RS): BO 2 sts, work to end.

NEXT ROW (WS): BO 4 sts, work to end.

NEXT ROW (RS): K1, ssk, work to end.

Rep last 2 rows 2 times—15 (19, 23, 27) sts.

FOR SIZE L AND XL

NEXT ROW (WS): BO 4 sts, work to end. Rep next WS row 0 (1) times—15 (19, 19, 19) sts.

NEXT RS ROW: Work to last 4 sts, k3tog, k1. Rep decs every RS row 4 (5, 5, 5) times—5 (7, 7, 7) sts.

NEXT RS ROW: Work to last 3 sts, k2tog, k1. Rep until 3 sts rem. BO.

LEFT SIDE

Attach yarn at left end and work WS row to end.

Complete as for right side, reversing all shaping. Substitute ssk for k2tog, and s2kp for k3tog.

TOP FRONT

Work as for back.

NECKLINE EDGING

Using 3.75mm circular and starting at right side of front, *pick up 30 (32, 36, 38) sts, pm, pick up 3 sts along top edge, pm, pick up 34 (36, 38, 40) sts, pm, pick up 34 (36, 38, 40) sts, pm, pick up 3 sts along top edge, pm, pick up 30 (32, 36, 38) sts, and rep from *.

Knit 1 row, inc 1 st after each marker. BO.

STRAPS

Using 3.75mm dpn, CO 2 sts and pick up 3 sts from top edge of bodice. Work I-cord for 7" and BO. Attach to top edge on back of bodice. Rep for other side.

silky NEGLIGEE

jessica thomaz

Whether you wear it on your wedding night or on a night in with takeout, you'll feel simply beautiful in this lacy nightgown. Demure in white or sexy in jewel tones and black, the color choice for the yarn and accompanying ribbon will make this design perfect for any occasion. Knit in a lightweight blend, tencel provides a silk-like sheen while keeping the care to a minimum.

SIZES

XS (S, M, L, XL)

30–33 (34–37, 38–41, 42–45, 46–49)"

Shown in size S

FINISHED MEASUREMENTS

unstretched

CHEST: 26 (30, 34, 38, 42)", unblocked

HIPS: 36 (41, 46, 51, 56)"

LENGTH FROM TOP EDGE TO BOTTOM EDGE: 29 (30, 31, 32, 33)"

YARN

Yarntini Merino/Tencel (50% superwash merino wool, 50% tencel; 490 yards/100g): 2 (3, 3, 4, 4) skeins, Port

NEEDLES

2.75mm circulars, 24" or 32" long

NOTIONS

¾" ribbon

Matching thread

7/16" button

Stitch marker

Tapestry needle

GAUGE

28 sts and 32 rows = 4" in St st

pattern notes

The first section of lace is knit flat using a circular needle. You will begin knitting in the round at the Stockinette stitch portion.

Jessica's obsession with yarn began on a move from Florida to Pennsylvania after college. The change in weather allowed her to finally indulge in most of the beautiful yarns available. Now, as the founder and dyer of Yarntini (www.yarntini.net), she's elbow deep in a dye pot and building the biggest yarn stash her wallet will allow.

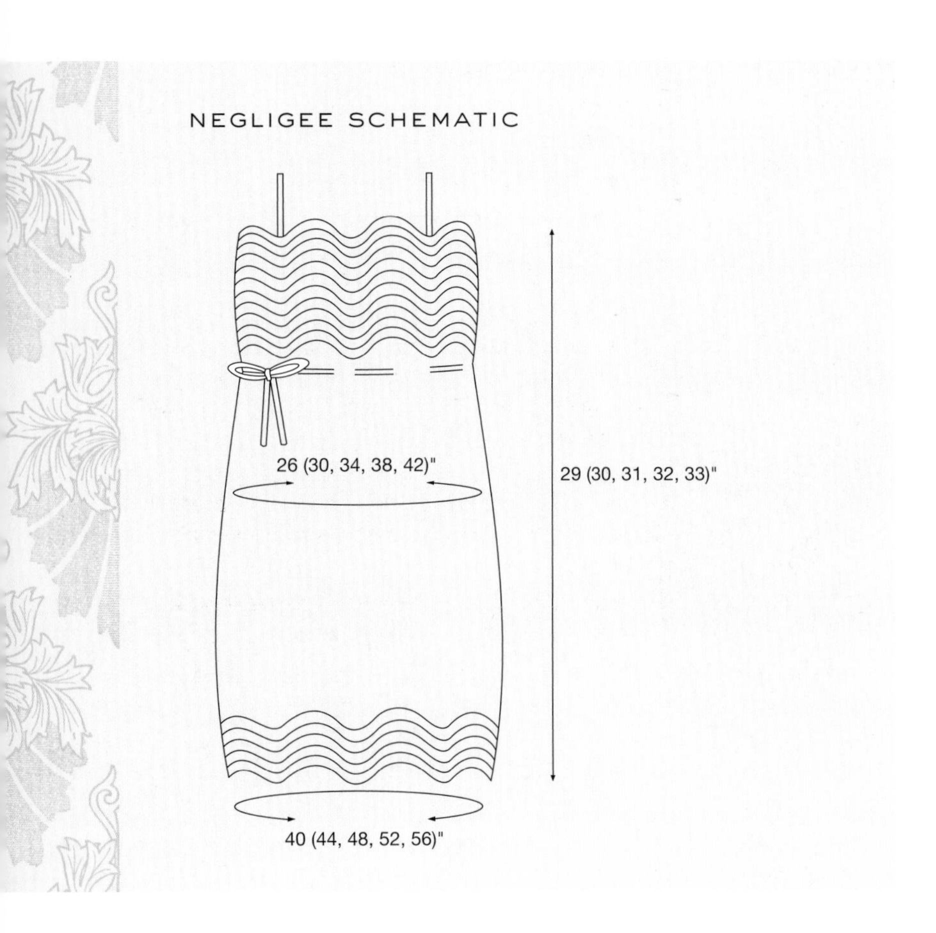

STITCH PATTERNS

LACE PATTERN (FLAT)

ROW 1: (K2tog) 3 times, *(k1, yo) 6 times, (k2tog) 6 times, rep from * to last 6 sts, (k2tog) 3 times.

ROW 2: Purl.

ROW 3: Knit.

ROW 4: Purl.

LACE PATTERN IN-THE-RND

ROW 1: (K2tog) 3 times, *(k1, yo) 6 times, (k2tog) 6 times, rep from * to last 6 sts, (k2tog) 3 times.

ROWS 2–4: Knit.

UPPER BODY

Using long-tail cast-on, CO 202 (238, 274, 310, 346) sts and work in Garter st for 2 rows. Begin lace patt, knitting the first and last 2 sts in each row, and work for 5½ (6, 6½, 7, 7½)", ending on Row 1 of lace patt. Work in Garter st for 2 rows.

NEXT RND (RS): Pm and join for working in the rnd, being careful not to twist sts.

Work in St st for 3 rnds.

EYELET RND: [K18 (15, 15, 15, 17), yo, k2tog] 10 (14, 16, 18, 18) times, knit to end of rnd. Work in St st for 3 rnds.

INCREASE RND: Using a M1 increase, inc 50 sts evenly over rnd—252 (288, 324, 360, 396) sts.

Work in St st until piece measures 23½ (24, 24½, 25, 25½)". Purl 2 rnds.

Beg lace patt in-the-rnd and work for 5½ (6, 6½, 7, 7½)", ending on Row 1 of lace patt. Purl 2 rnds.

BO loosely.

FINISHING

Wet block to desired measurement, pinning out lace pattern to accentuate the scalloped edges.

Weave in end of yarn at bottom edge.

Using tail end of yarn at top corner, make loop large enough to hold button and secure. Attach button to opposite side using scrap yarn.

With matching thread, attach two strips of ribbon to inside back edge, each one approximately 2" in from button and button loop. Make sure to place them on a "bump" rather than a "dip" in scalloped edge to preserve shape.

While trying on gown, pin fronts of straps so that they are the perfect length, remembering to attach to a "bump." Sew front of straps to inside front edge.

Weave ribbon through eyelet holes, cut to your preferred length, and tie in a bow.

ivy DRESS

sauniell n. connally

Designed in the spirit of a traditional gown, the elegance of Ivy is achieved in the lace detail and shaping. The skirt shaping lends for a sleek, straight look in the front but gives proper ease for the hips in the back. A lace leaf vine pattern highlights the sash and enhances the sleek look of the skirt. The wool/silk blend provides the perfect balance of luster and structure to this gown.

SIZES

XS (S, M, L, XL)

28–30 (32–34, 36–38, 40–42, 44–46)"

Shown in size S

FINISHED MEASUREMENTS

unstretched

BUST: 30½ (34, 36, 40, 43)"

HIP: 42 (44, 47, 49, 53)"

YARN

Louisa Harding Grace Silk & Wool (50% merino wool, 50% silk; 110 yards/50g): 14 (15, 18, 20, 22) skeins, Tan (02)

NEEDLES

4mm circulars, 32" long

4mm straight needles

4mm dpns

NOTIONS

Stitch markers

Stitch holder

Tapestry needle

GAUGE

22 sts and 30 rows = 4" in St st

pattern notes

Stitch count for Lace Leaf Vine varies from row to row, but begins and ends with 26 stitches.

When working the lace panel chart for the sash, Row 1 is worked on the wrong side (WS) and starts on the left.

When working skirt in the round, chart is worked from right to left on every round, using legend definitions for right side (RS) knitting.

Sauniell's designs have appeared in knit simple *and* knit 1 *as well as the web knitting magazine Magknits.com. She believes in designing fashionable yet classic items, and will not design anything she would not wear herself. Visit her blog at saunshine.blogspot.com.*

STITCH PATTERNS

s2kp — slip 2 sts, k1, pass slipped sts over

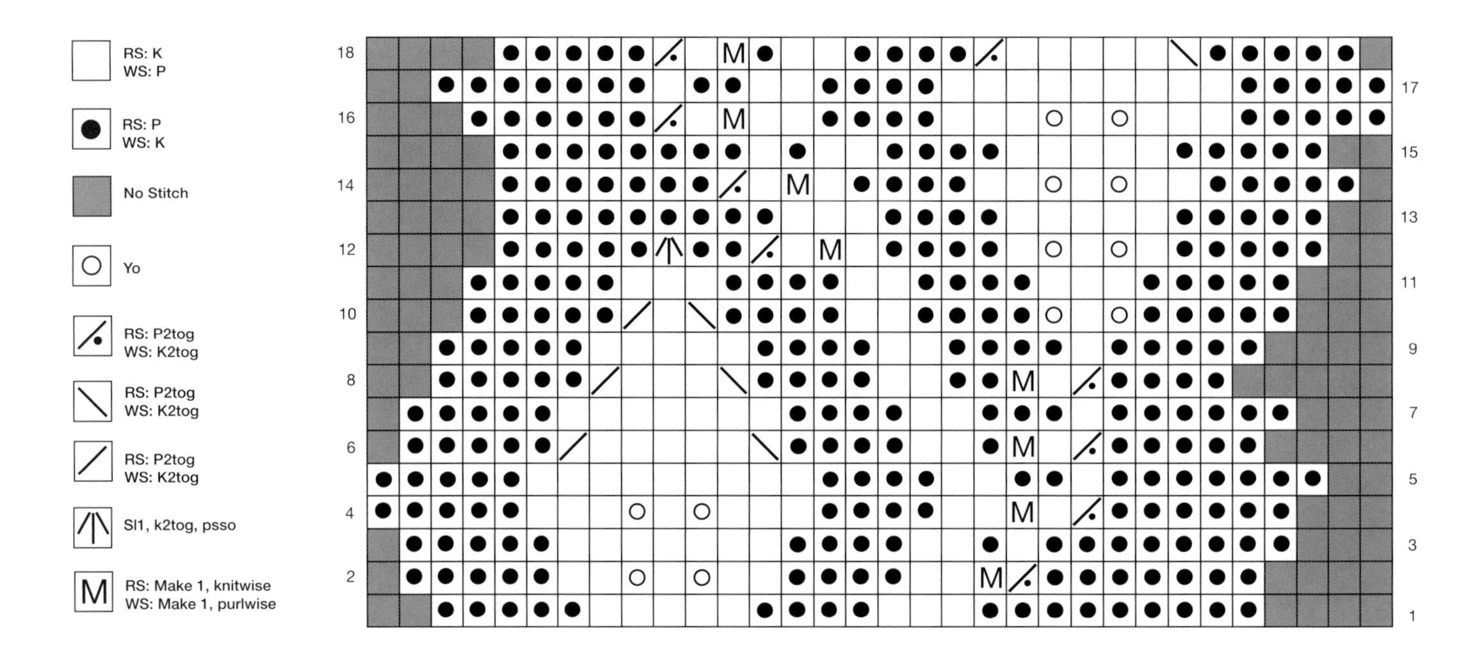

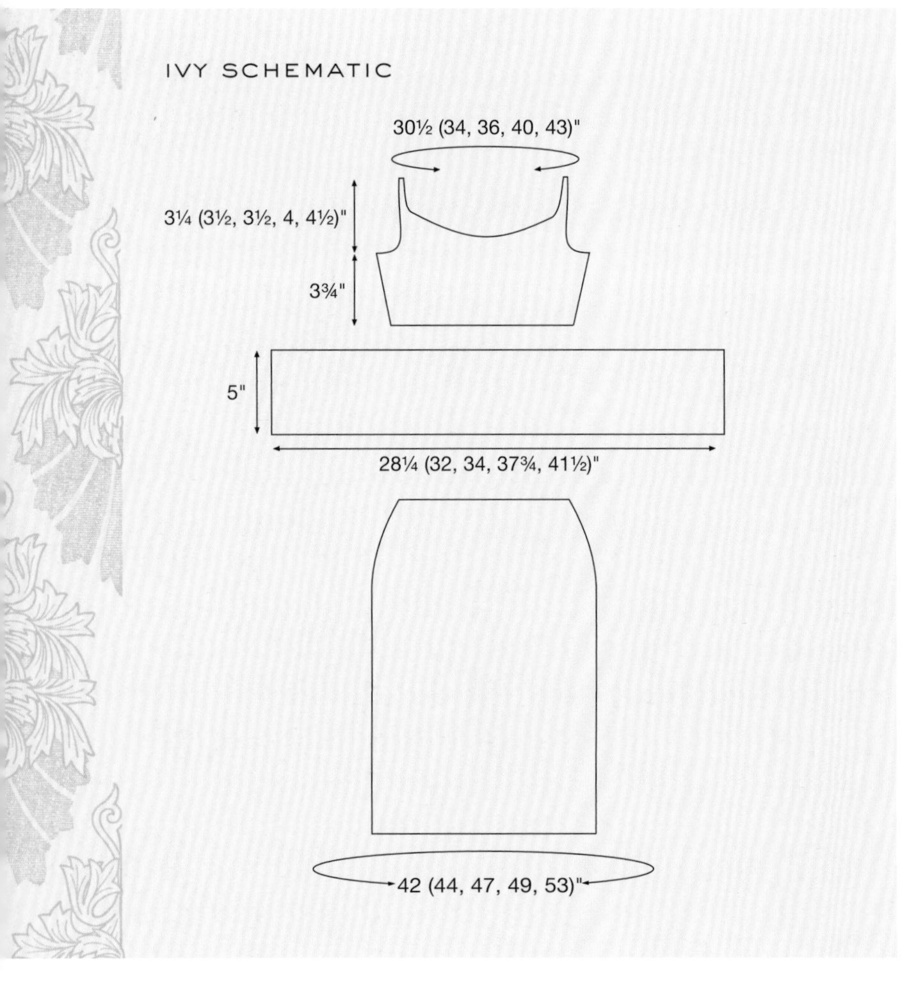

SASH

Using 4mm needles, CO 30 sts and knit 1 row.

NEXT ROW (WS): P2, work Row 1 of Lace Leaf Vine patt, p2.

NEXT ROW (RS): K2, work Row 2 of Lace Leaf Vine patt, k2.

Cont to work as set, repeating patt a total of 8 (10, 10, 11, 13) times. Then work 14 (0, 10, 16, 0) rows of patt. Knit 1 row and BO. Sew cast-on and BO edges together.

BODICE

Using 4mm circular needles and starting at center back seam of sash, pick up 39 (44, 47, 52, 57) sts, pm, pick up 78 (88, 94, 104, 114) sts, pm, and pick up 39 (44, 47, 52, 57) sts—156 (176, 188, 208, 228) sts. Knit 2 rnds.

NEXT RND: *K to 1st marker, inc 1, k1, sm, k1, inc 1, and rep from * one time, then knit to end of rnd. Rep incs EOR 2 times—168 (188, 200, 220, 240) sts. Work as set for 20 rnds.

NEXT RND: *Knit to 5 sts before marker, BO 10 sts, rep from * once, knit to end of rnd. Break yarn. Place front sts on st holder.

TOP BACK

Attach yarn at right armhole edge and work as foll:

NEXT ROW (RS): K2, ssk, work to last 4 sts, k2tog, k2.

NEXT ROW (WS): P2, p2tog, purl to last 4 sts, p2tog tbl, p2. Rep last 2 rows 2 (2, 2, 3, 3) times—62 (72, 78, 84, 94) sts.

Continue working sides separately, working first 31 (36, 39, 42, 47) sts on needle.

RIGHT SIDE

NEXT ROW (RS): K1, ssk, k to last 4, k3tog, k1.

NEXT ROW (WS): P1, p2tog, purl to last 3 sts, p2tog tbl, p1. Rep last 2 rows 2 (3, 4, 4, 5) times—16 (16, 14, 17, 17) sts.

NEXT ROW: K to last 4 sts, k3tog, k1. Rep EOR 5 (5, 4, 5, 5) times—4 (4, 4, 5, 5) sts.

NEXT ROW (RS): K to last 3 sts, k2tog, k1. Rep EOR row 0 (0, 0, 1, 1) times. Work WS row and BO.

LEFT SIDE

Attach yarn at center back and work complete as for right side, reversing all shaping. Substitute ssk for k2tog, and s2kp for k3tog.

TOP FRONT

Work as for back.

NECKLINE EDGING

Using 4mm circular and starting at right side of front, *pick up 26 (27, 28, 33, 35) sts, pm, pick up 3 sts along top edge, pm, pick up 16(18, 20, 22, 24) sts down right neck edge, pm, pick up 16(18, 20, 22, 24) sts up left neck edge, pm, pick up 3 sts along top edge, pm, pick up 26 (27, 28, 33, 35) sts down left side of front, and rep from *.

Knit 1 row, inc 1 st after each marker. BO.

SKIRT

Using 4mm circular needles and starting at center back seam of sash, pick up 39 (44, 47, 52, 57), pm, pick up 78 (88, 94, 104, 114), pm, and pick up 39 (44, 47, 52, 57), pm—156 (176, 188, 196, 208, 228) sts.

NEXT RND: K to mkr, sm, k26 (31, 34, 39, 44) sts, work Row 1 Lace Leaf Vine patt for circular knitting, and knit to end of rnd. Cont in patt for 4 rnds.

INC RND: K2, inc 1, work to 1 st before marker, inc1, k1, sm, work in patt to next mkr, sm, k1, inc 1, knit to 2 sts before end of rnd, inc 1, k2.

Rep Inc Rnd every 4th rnd 9 times, then EOR 3 (1, 1, 1, 2) times. Work 1 rnd—208 (220, 232, 252, 276) sts.

NEXT RND: K2, inc 1, work to last 2 sts of the rnd, inc 1, k2. Rep EOR 10 (10, 12, 8, 8) times. Continue until skirt measures 32" (approx 10 patt reps) from bottom of sash or to desired length.

NEXT RND: Purl to lace leaf section, work in patt, purl to end. Rep EOR 2 times.

NEXT RND: Purl all sts in rnd. Knit 1 rnd. Rep last 2 rnds 2 times and BO.

STRAPS (MAKE 2)

Using 4mm dpn, pick up 3 sts from top edge of bodice and CO 2 sts. Work 5-st I-cord (see Special Techniques, page 137) for 7" and BO. Attach to top edge on back of bodice.

FINISHING

Weave in ends.

CHAPTER FIVE

MAGIC IS IN THE DETAILS

accessories to complete the look

lily-of-the-valley OPERA GLOVES

olga buraya-kefelian

Like a garden in the spring, these gloves mirror the exquisiteness of the sweet, romantic flower—the lily-of-the-valley. Their elegant, austere beauty could melt the heart of an ice princess. The lace creates a unique look suitable for special occasions, or to accent a cool-season outfit. Knit up from a luxurious combination of wool and silk, they will keep your arms not only warmed, but infinitely caressed. The gloves are worked in the round and adorned with a picot hem.

SIZE

FINISHED MEASUREMENTS

HAND CIRCUMFERENCE: 6¾ (7, 7½, 7¾, 8)"

ELBOW CIRCUMFERENCE: 8¾ (9, 9¼, 9¾, 10)"

LENGTH: 19¾" for all sizes

YARN

Habu 3/15 Silk Wool (70% wool, 30% silk; 270 yards/50g): 2 skeins, white

NEEDLES

2.75mm dpns

NOTIONS

Two stitch holders

Stitch markers

Scrap yarn

Tapestry needle

GAUGE

36 sts and 40 rows = 4" in St st

pattern notes

Work lace chart (16 rows) for 10 full repeats. Work final (11th) repeat through Row 13, continuing in Stockinette stitch until desired length to fingers.

Use backward loop cast-on method when adding new stitches for fingers.

Try on glove as you knit each finger, adjusting length of fingers as needed.

Olga has been knitting since the age of four and has been creating her own garments for the past nine years. She enjoys the challenge that each garment brings and acquires her inspiration from current runway trends. She lives with her husband and crazy cat in Alexandria, Virginia. You can see more of her everyday knitwear adventures at www.olgajazzy.com.

STITCH PATTERN

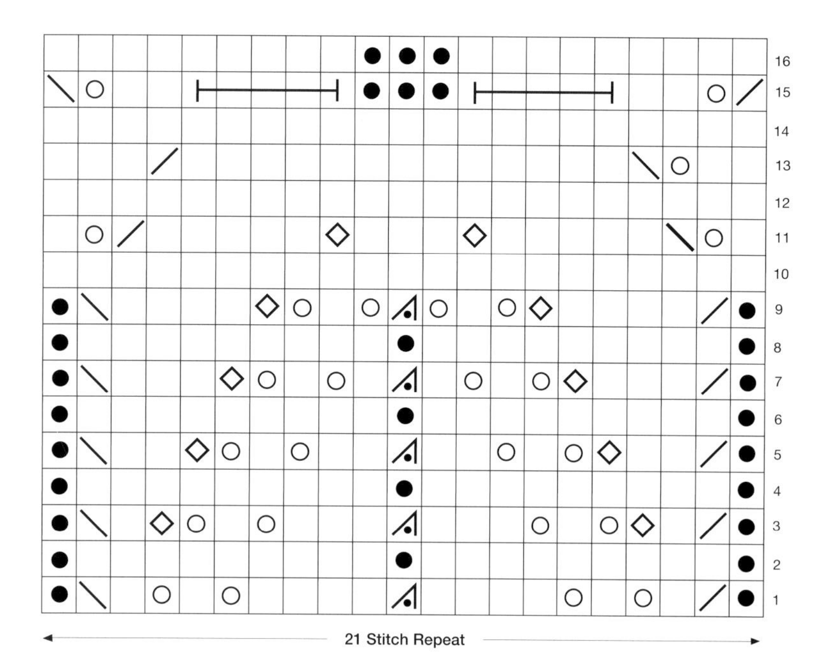

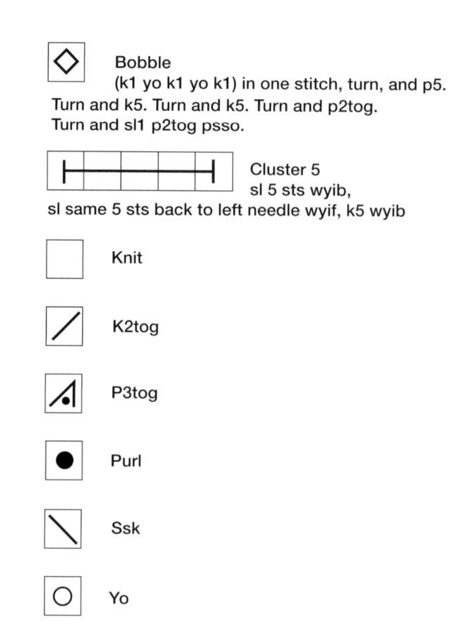

RIGHT GLOVE

Using a provisional cast-on, CO 78 (81, 84, 87, 90) sts; divide evenly on 3 needles. Join for working in the rnd, being careful not to twist, and pm for beg of rnd. Knit 8 rnds, then work 1 picot turn rnd as foll: K1, *k2tog, yo; rep from * to end of rnd. Knit 8 more rnds. Turn hem and sew in place.

Knit 4 rnds.

DEC RND: K27 (28, 29, 30, 31) sts, ssk, work Row 1 of Lace Panel chart over next 21 sts, k2tog, k24 (26, 28, 30, 32) sts, k2tog—3 sts decreased. Work even in patt as established for 10 rnds. Rep last 11 rnds 8 times, cont decs 1 sts before and after lace panel and 1 st before beg of rnd marker—51 (54, 57, 59, 64) sts rem.

Work even in patt for 3".

INC RND: Work to 1 st before lace panel, k1fb, work Lace Panel as established, k1fb, work to last st, k1fb—57 (60, 63, 66, 69) sts. Work even in patt for 1".

*Work to 1 st before Lace Panel, k1fb, work lace panel as established, k1fb, work to end of rnd (omit last inc). Work even in patt for 1"

Repeat from * one more time.

THUMB INSET

Knit to 5 (6, 6, 7, 7) sts after Lace Panel, pm for side center. With a 15" piece of contrasting waste yarn k9 (10, 10, 11, 11) sts. Sl worked sts back onto LH needle and knit them with working yarn.

Work even for 1¾". AT THE SAME TIME, end final repeat of Lace Panel chart with Row 13, knitting any additional rows.

Divide sts as evenly as possible between two st holders, putting any extra (odd) sts on top stitch holder. Do not break yarn.

THUMB

Carefully remove contrasting waste yarn and place live sts on two dpns side by side; 9 (10, 10, 11, 11) sts below opening on one needle and 10 (11, 11, 12, 12) sts above opening on second needle. Attach yarn and pick up 2 new sts at side of thumb, knit sts on needle below opening, pick up 4 new sts at other side of thumb, knit sts on needle above opening, pick up 2 more new sts at side of thumb—27 (29, 29, 31, 31) sts.

Work even for ¾".

NEXT RND: K2tog at back of thumb—26 (28, 28, 30, 30) sts.

Work even for 1¼" and next rnd k2tog at front of thumb—25 (27, 27, 29, 29) sts rem.

Work even until thumb is desired length.

NEXT RND: K2tog to last st, k1.

Pull yarn through rem sts.

INDEX FINGER

Beg at side edge, k9 (9, 9, 10, 10) sts from holder, using backward loop method, CO 4 sts, k9 (9, 10, 10, 11) sts from opposite holder—22 (22, 23, 24, 25) sts.

Work even for 1½" from the side CO sts.

NEXT RND: K2tog at back of finger—21 (21, 22, 23, 24) sts rem.

Work for ¾" and next rnd k2tog at front of finger—21 (21, 22, 23, 24) sts rem.

Work even until index finger is desired length.

NEXT RND: K2tog to end.

Pull yarn through rem sts.

MIDDLE FINGER

Starting next to index finger, k7 (8, 8, 9, 9) sts from holder, CO 4 sts, k7 (8, 8, 8, 9) sts from opposite holder, pick up new 4 sts from index finger CO sts—23 (24, 24, 25, 26) sts.

Work even for 2".

NEXT RND: K2tog at back of finger—22 (23, 23, 24, 25) sts.

Work even for ¾" and next rnd k2tog in front of finger—21 (22, 22, 23, 24) sts rem.

Work even until middle finger is desired length.

NEXT RND: K2tog to end.

Pull yarn through rem sts.

RING FINGER

Starting next to middle finger, k7 (7, 8, 8, 8) sts from holder, CO 4 sts, k6 (7, 7, 8, 9) sts from opposite holder, pick up 4 new sts from middle finger CO sts—21 (22, 23, 24, 25) sts.

Work even for 2".

NEXT RND: K2tog at back of finger 20—(21, 22, 23, 24) sts.

Work even for ¾" and next rnd k2tog in front of finger—19 (21, 21, 22, 23) sts.

Work even until ring finger is desired length.

NEXT RND: K2tog to end.

Pull yarn through rem sts.

LITTLE FINGER

Sl rem sts from each holder onto separate needles. Starting next to ring finger, k7 (8, 8, 8, 9) sts from first holder, then k8 (8, 9, 9, 8) sts from opposite holder, pick up 4 new sts from ring finger CO sts—19 (20, 21, 21, 21) sts.

Work even for 1¾".

NEXT RND: K2tog at back of finger—18 (19, 20, 20, 20) sts.

Work even until little finger is desired length.

NEXT RND: K2tog to end.

Pull yarn through rem sts.

FINISHING

Pull yarn to inside of each finger, weave ends in securely.

LEFT GLOVE

Work as for right glove until Thumb Inset Rnd.

Knit to 26 (27, 30, 31, 34) sts after Lace Panel, k9 (10, 10, 11, 11) sts with a 15" piece of a contrasting yarn, then slip them back onto LH needle and knit them with the main color yarn, pm.

Work even for 1¾".

Complete as for right glove.

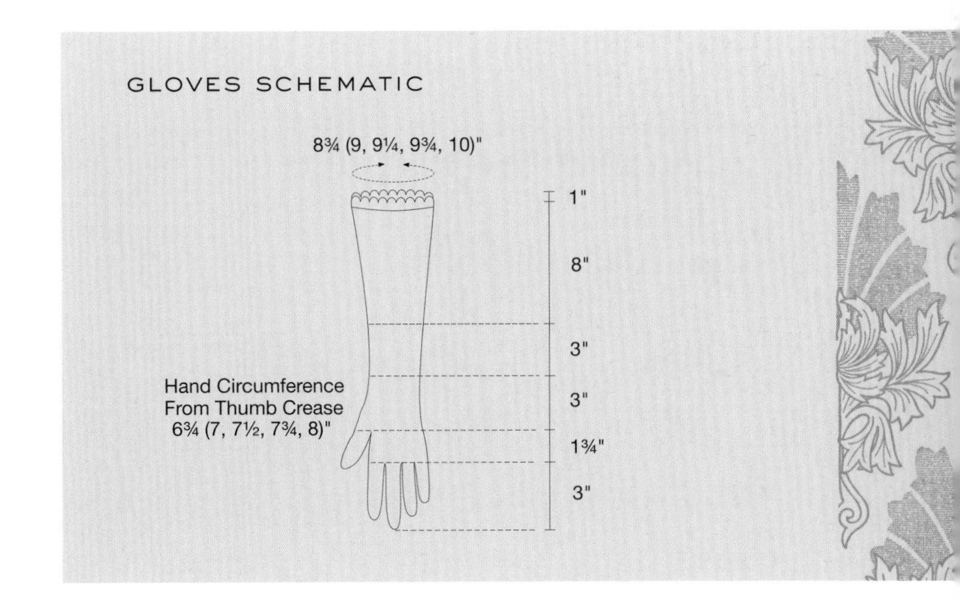

cleopatra WRAP

miriam l. felton

The Cleopatra Wrap evokes the mystery and beauty of ancient Egypt, where women like Cleopatra wore gossamer thin pleated robes. The lace detail on each end of the wrap recalls the fluted lotus-topped columns that adorned Egypt's great temples in the desert.

SIZE

ONE SIZE

FINISHED MEASUREMENTS

unstretched

16" wide x 80" long

YARN

Pure Knits Bamboo Laceweight (100% bamboo; 676 yards/55g): 2 skeins, Mulberry

NEEDLES

3.25mm straight or circulars

If using circular needles, you will need an extra circular in same size to hold sts while grafting.

NOTIONS

Tapestry needle

GAUGE

36 sts and 40 rows = 4" in St st

pattern notes

The wrap is worked in two pieces and grafted together at the center to make the lace edges match.

Odd numbered rows are right side and even numbered rows are wrong side.

All wrong side rows are purled with the first and last 3 stitches in Seed stitch.

Miriam lives with her long-suffering husband and cat in Salt Lake City. She has had patterns published by Knit Picks, Interweave Knits, *and runs her own self-publishing business. You can find more lace and historically inspired knits at her web site, www.mimknits.com and tutorials and discussion on knitting on her blog at www.mimknits.com/wordpress.*

STITCH PATTERN

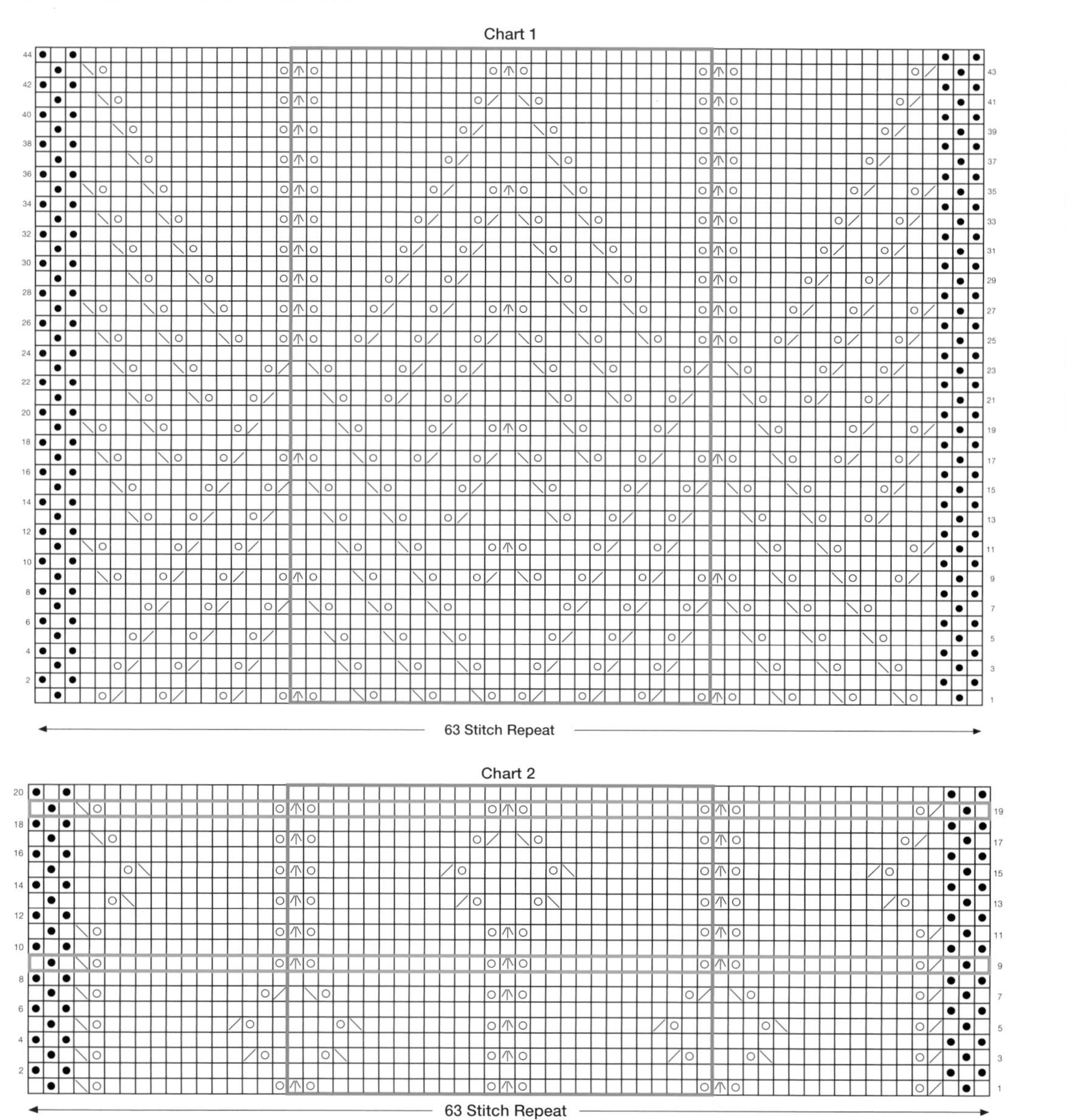

Highlighted rows to be repeated 12 times each within 20 row pattern repeat

WRAP PART 1

Cast on 119 sts.

ROWS 1–3: *K1, p1; rep to last st, k1.

Begin lace patt, following Chart 1 with Row 1.

When Chart 1 is finished, transfer live sts to spare needle and set aside.

WRAP PART 2

Repeat as above for second side of wrap.

When Rows 1–44 of Chart 1 are completed, begin Chart 2. (Be sure to repeat Rows 9 and 19 a total of 12 times each.)

Repeat Rows 1–20 of Chart 2 (including additional reps of Rows 9 and 19) until piece measures 74" lightly stretched, ending with Row 9 (without repeats).

ASSEMBLY

Break yarn, leaving tail 4 times width of wrap. Place Part 1 and Part 2 with wrong sides facing. Graft both pieces together using Kitchener st (see Special Techniques, page 137), being careful not to pull working yarn too tightly.

FINISHING

Weave in ends, but do not trim.

Spray lightly with water and spread to finished measurements, opening up the lace. Tension is not necessary. Be careful, as bamboo fiber is weaker when wet. You may wish to pin the points of the edging before spraying to make a nice, crisp edge.

loop SHAWL

leah bear

Wrap yourself in luxury and style with this cable and lace shawl. Knit flat and seamed, the unique loop construction makes this a "go everywhere" piece. This exquisite, light and airy angora knit is easily worn as a shawl, scarf, or anything else you can dream up. The versatility of the design paired with the lush fiber will make this a must have for seasons to come.

SIZE

ONE SIZE

FINISHED MEASUREMENTS

unstretched

12" x 80" before blocking

14" x 80" after blocking

YARN

Louisa Harding Kimono Angora Pure (70% angora, 25% wool, 5% nylon; 125 yards/25g): 5 skeins, Black (#8)

NEEDLES

4.5mm straight needles

NOTIONS

Tapestry needle

Cable needle

Scrap yarn

Blocking pins

GAUGE

20 sts and 30 rows = 4" in St st

pattern notes

This pattern uses a provisional cast-on and Kitchener st (see Special Techniques, page 137).

Chart reflects one pattern repeat with a knitted selvage stitch on either side. Please note that the number of stitches alternates row to row.

Leah lives with her husband in Atlanta. She is a certified behavior analyst who works with children with disabilities. When she's not knitting, she can be found in the kitchen channeling Julia Child, hitting the road, or typing all about it on her blog, www.betweenstupidandclever.com.

STITCH PATTERN

TWISTED CABLE FRONT (TCF): sl 3 sts to cable needle and hold to front of work, k3, k3tog tbl from cable needle

TWISTED CABLE BACK (TCB): sl 3 sts to cable needle and hold to back of work, k3tog tbl, k3 from the cable needle

SHAWL

Using provisional cast-on, CO 58 sts loosely.

The lace patt consists of 12 rows. Purl all WS rows. Repeat these 12 rows until piece measures 80" (or desired length). Do not cast off.

Leaving 25" of yarn for grafting, place live sts on scrap yarn and secure.

FINISHING

Weave in all loose ends (except for grafting yarn) and block shawl lightly to open lace patt.

After blocking, place both ends of shawl (the cast-on and the live sts) back on needles. Graft together using Kitchener st. Cut excess yarn and weave in ends.

Block grafted area.

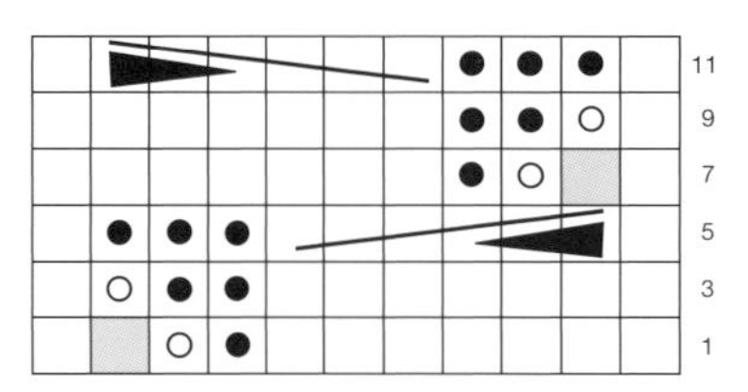

Loop Shawl Lace Chart

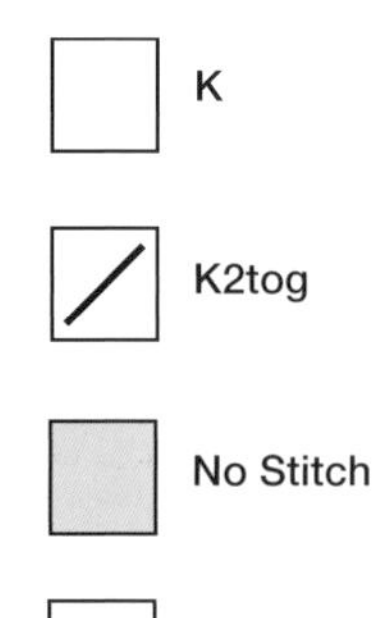

(Twisted Cable Front): Hold 3 stitches on the cable needle in front of work, k3tog, and then work the three stitches from the cable needle together by knitting into the back of the stitches.

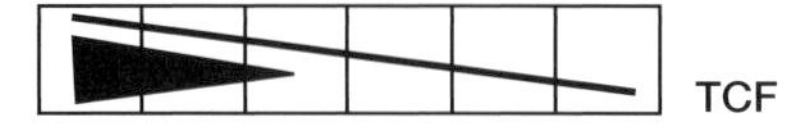

(Twisted Cable Back): Hold 3 stitches on the cable needle in the back of the work, k3tog by knitting into the back of the work, and then knit the three stitches from the cable needle.

adelle STOCKINGS

rangsiwan fasudhani

Enjoy tiptoeing around in the morning or cozying up at night in this classic pair of stockings. Worked toe-up using the magic loop method, these stockings are knit in a stretchy lace pattern that does not require any shaping until after the knee. Elastic knit into the cuff helps keep the stockings up, while a patterned toe gives them a beautiful, finished look.

SIZE

FITS WOMEN'S SHOE SIZE 8–9

FINISHED MEASUREMENTS

CALF CIRCUMFERENCE: Up to 14½" (stretched)

THIGH CIRCUMFERENCE: Up to 18" (stretched)

LENGTH: 22" cuff to top of heel (unstretched)

FOOT: 3½" (unstretched)

LEG: 3¼" (unstretched)

WIDEST PART OF THIGH: 5" (unstretched)

YARN

Posh Yarn Lucia (70% merino, 30% cashmere; 360 yards/100g): 2 skeins, Slate

NEEDLES

2.75mm circulars, 29" long

NOTIONS

Rainbow 1mm fine Elastic

GAUGE

28 sts and 36 rows = 4" in St st

pattern notes

Two rounds of the lace pattern require that you move one stitch back and forth between needles. Do this on even rounds to minimize dropped stitches.

Move first stitch of Needle 2 to Needle 1 as foll: Work Needle 1 and turn. Work first st on Needle 2 and pull needle towards you to allow st just worked to slide down cord, meeting with sts on Needle 1. Work to end.

Move last st of Needle 1 to Needle 2 as foll: Work to last st on Needle 1. Pull needle towards you to allow st just worked to slide down cord, meeting with sts on Needle 2. Turn and work to end.

Rangsiwan was born, raised and is currently living in San Francisco, California. On a mission to save money on holiday gifts, she started knitting with her best friend in 2003. She now tries to balance her time between knitting, sewing, cooking, baking, and maintaining her day job. You can read more about her crafty adventures at www.yaiann.com.

STITCH PATTERN

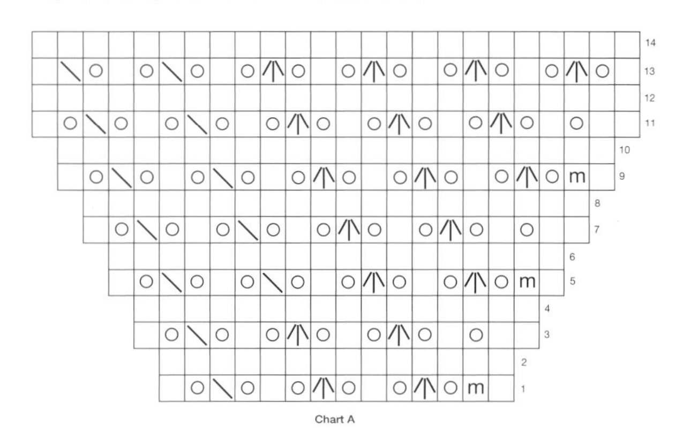

Chart A

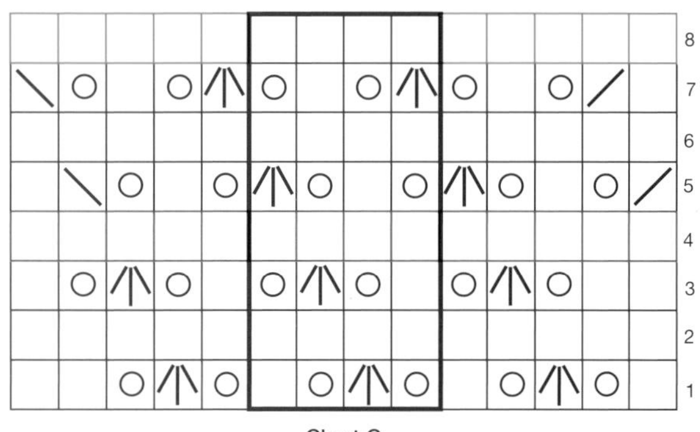

Chart C

TOE

Using the Turkish cast-on method (see Special Techniques, page 139), CO 24 sts, 12 on each needle.

NEEDLE 1: Work chart A.

NEEDLE 2: K1, m1, knit to last st, m1, k1. Next row, knit. Rep these two rows until 26 stitches on needles (50 st, 24 on Needle 1, 26 on Needle 2).

FOOT

NEEDLE 1: Work chart B.

NEEDLE 2: Knit all sts. Continue working chart B for instep on Needle 1 and St st on Needle 2 for sole. Rep until foot measures 7½" or 2" less than desired length, ending with Row 3 on Needle 1.

HEEL

Heel sts will be worked back and forth on Needle 2.

ROW 1: Knit 25 stitches, w/t (see Special Techniques, page 138).

ROW 2: Purl 24 stitches, w/t.

ROW 3: Knit to one st before wrapped st, w/t.

ROW 4: Purl to one st before wrapped st, w/t.

Rep Rows 3 and 4 until 7 total sts have been wrapped on each side.

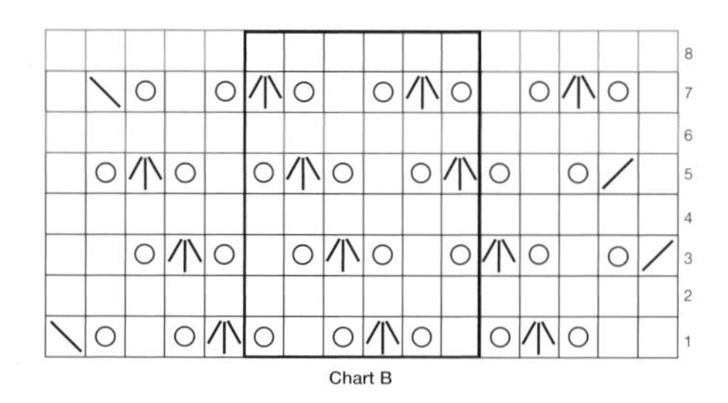

Chart B

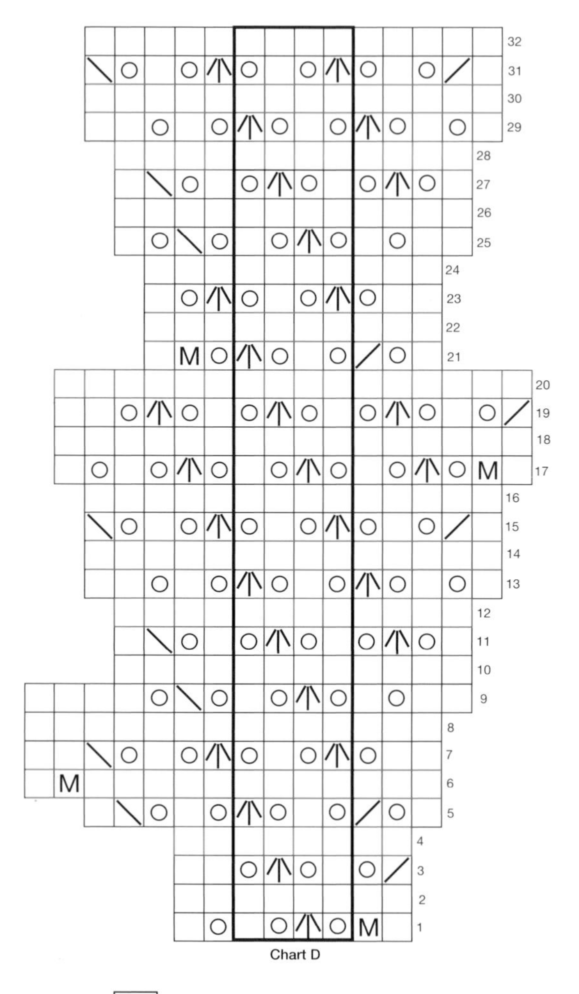

Chart D

- K
- Yo
- Ssk
- K2tog
- Sl1, k2tog, psso

ROW 1: Knit to first wrapped st. Insert needle into wrap from below and then into st. Knit st and wrap together, w/t. (The st just wrapped will now have two wraps.)

ROW 2: Purl to first wrapped st. Insert needle into wrap from behind and then into st. Purl st and wrap together, w/t.

ROW 3: Knit to double wrapped st. Insert needle into both wraps from below and then into st. Knit st and wraps together, w/t.

ROW 4: Purl to double wrapped st. Insert needle into both wraps from behind and then into st. Purl st and wraps together, w/t.

Rep Rows 3 and 4 until all wraps have been picked up, ending with a WS row. Turn work so RS is facing.

Resume knitting in the rnd.

NEEDLE 1: Knit

NEEDLE 2: K13.

Rearrange sts on needle so that each needle has 13 heel sts and 12 instep sts. Do this by pinching cord between 12th and 13th st on Needle 1. Slowly pull cord from between sts allowing the 13 heel and 12 instep sts to come together on each needle. The rnd will now begin at center of back of leg, above heel.

LEG

Beg Chart C and rep until leg measures 16" from top of heel, or until stocking reaches top of knee.

THIGH

Work Chart D, (66 st). Work two reps of Chart C or until stocking measures 1½" less than desired length.

CUFF

Cuff will be worked alternating with yarn and elastic held together and yarn held by itself, stranding the elastic behind. Knit one rnd, inc 1 st at beg and end of rnd with yarn only (68 st).

Work k2, p2 rib as foll: *K2 with yarn only, p2 with yarn and elastic held together, rep from * to end of rnd. Work a total of 15 rnds or for 1½". BO in patt with yarn only.

Repeat for second stocking.

ABBREVIATIONS

beg	begin(ing)
bet	between
BO	bind off (UK: cast off)
CC	contrast color
cn	cable needle
CO	cast on
cont	continue(ing)
dec	decrease(ing)
dpn	double pointed needle(s)
EOR	every other row
inc	increase(ing)
k	knit
k2tog	knit two together
k1fb	knit into front and back
LH	left hand
M1	make 1, increase
M1L	lift strand bet two needles from front to back with LH needle; knit it through front loop
MIR	lift strand bet two needles from back to front with LH needle; knit it through back loop
MC	main color
p	purl
p1fb	purl into front and back
p1bf	purl into back and front
p2tog	purl 2 together
p2tog tbl	insert right needle up into back loops of the two stitches and purl them together from this position
patt	pattern
pm	place marker
RH	right hand
RS	right side
rem	remaining
rep	repeat
rnd(s)	round(s)
sl	slip
sm	slip marker
ssk	slip 2 stitches as if to knit, knit 2 stitches together on LH
ssp	sl 1 knitwise, slip another knitwise; return slipped sts to left needle
st(s)	stitch(es)
St st	stockinette stitch
tbl	through back loop
wyib	with yarn in back
wyif	with yarn in front
WS	wrong side
w/t	wrap and turn
yo	yarn over
*	rep directions from *
**	rep directions between ** as directed

KNITTING NEEDLE CONVERSION

Metric (mm)	US	UK/Canada
2.0	0	14
2.25	1	13
2.75	2	12
3.0	-	11
3.25	3	10
3.5	4	-
3.75	5	9
4.0	6	8
4.5	7	7
5.0	8	6
5.5	9	5
6.0	10	4
6.5	10½	3
7.0	-	2
7.5	-	1
8.0	11	0
9.0	13	00
10.0	15	000

SPECIAL TECHNIQUES

What follows are some of the techniques used in this book. This isn't a comprehensive guide, but rather a quick and convenient reference to particular techniques that may not be found in other books or where I wanted to show my favorite way of executing the technique.

BACKWARD LOOP CO

*Loop working yarn and place it on the needle backwards so that it doesn't unwind. Rep from * for specified number of stitches.

I-CORD

Using dpns or circular needles, CO or p/u req sts.

*Knit a row. Slide row to other end of needle. Do not turn the work. Pull the yarn around the back of stitches. Rep from *.

INTARSIA

In intarsia, blocks of color are worked with different lengths of yarn. The yarns are not carried across the back of work when not in use. To prevent holes, twist the yarn by picking up the new color from under the old color.

INVISIBLE OR PROVISIONAL CO

There are several ways to perform an invisible or provisional cast-on. My preferred way is the chained version because it's quick and painless with no stitches to pick up. It's perfect to use with tubular cast-ons. I'll admit, though, that for hems I sometimes simply cast onto two same-sized needles, leave one hanging, and when it's time to knit the stitches together I already have them on a needle.

Using same needle size as used for work and cotton scrap yarn, make a slip knot onto your crochet hook. *Holding the knitting needle over scrap yarn on your left hand, bring the hook over your needle and crochet a chain stitch. Move yarn back under knitting needle. Repeat from * for required cast-on amount.

KITCHENER STITCH

The trick to this invisible grafting method is to repeat in your head "knit purl, purl knit" as you weave the live stitches. Thread a darning needle with a length of yarn that is twice as long as the join. Hold the needles parallel, tips pointing in same direction, and wrong sides of work together.

Set-up: Insert darning needle into the first st on the front needle as if to purl and pull through, leave the st on the needle.

Insert darning needle into the first st on the back needle as if to knit and pull through, leave the st on the needle.

Repeats: *Insert needle into the first st on the front needle as if to knit, remove st from needle.

Insert needle into the next st on the front needle as if to purl, leave st on the needle. Draw yarn through.

Insert needle into the first st on the back needle as if to purl, remove st from needle.

Insert needle into the next st on the back needle as if to knit, leave st on the needle. Draw yarn through.

Rep from * until no sts remain.

MAGIC LOOP METHOD (SMALL CIRCUMFERENCE KNITTING)

This is a great way to knit socks or sleeves in the round if you don't like to use dpns or very short circulars. You'll need 32" or longer circulars for this technique.

Using a circular needle, cast on the required number of stitches. Slide the stitches to the cable, pinch the cable between the two center stitches and pull it out to create a large loop. Half the stitches will be on one needle and the other half are on the second needle. This is called "home position."

With needle tips pointing to the right, slide back needle out (stitches will be on cable) and start knitting the stitches on the front needle as usual.

At the end of the row (half the round has been completed) turn the work around and return the stitches to home position. The stitches you're about to knit are in front (closest to you) and the yarn attached to the skein is on the right side of the needle in back.

Repeat, returning to home position and knitting the stitches in front until all rounds have been completed.

MATTRESS STITCH

Also known as invisible seaming, use mattress stitch to join vertical pieces together for a continous look. It is worked one stitch in from the edge. To begin, lay the two pieces side by side with RS up and thread a darning needle with same yarn as used in work. Insert the needle into the lowest corner stitch on the left piece from back to front. Then insert the needle from back to front in the lowest corner stitch on the opposite piece. You have tacked down the yarn and are ready to seam.

Stretch your work a little and you'll see a bar between the stitches. Insert the needle under the first two bars and pull through to the RS again. Insert the needle through the parallel bars on opposite piece. Continue working back and forth in this manner, gently pulling yarn sometimes to bring seam together, until you reach end.

SHORT ROW SHAPING

Short row, also known as wrap and turn, is used to shape or curve sections of knitting like heels of socks, shoulders, or collars.

Work to required number of stitches, wrap and turn (w/t):

Slip stitch from LH purlwise to RH needle, bring working yarn to front, slip stitch back to LH, and turn work.

Once the number of rows in your pattern is completed you must hide the wraps. The standard way to is pick up the wrap from beneath (or from above if it is on the purl side) and knit (or purl) it with the wrapped stitch.

My friend Joelene taught me an even better way that insures you'll end up with matching sides and no holes: Pick up the wrap from the bottom and slip on RH needle. Knit the wrapped stitch and pass the slipped stitch over. Wrap next stitch (this stitch will now have two wraps).

On purl side, pick up the wrap on the knit side bottom up and slip on RH needle. Purl wrapped stitch, pass slipped stich over, and wrap next stitch.

Repeat process, picking up and passing two wraps, until all stitches are reincorporated.

SHOULDER SHAPING

For a beautiful, less-bulky shoulder seam, combine short rows with a three-needle bind-off. When the pattern has you binding off in steps, work short rows instead. The trick is to remember is that the right front and left back shoulders are worked with knit side short rows, while the left front and right back shoulders are worked with purl side short rows. Work one additional row before starting the shoulder shaping and work a row to pick up the wraps.

Instead of binding off the pattern stitches, leave those stitches unworked, turning the short row at that spot. For example, if the pattern tells you to BO 5 stitches, then work until there are 5 stitches on LH needle, w/t.

THREE-NEEDLE BIND-OFF

With stitches on two same-sized needles and right sides facing, hold the two needles in your LH and insert a third needle into the first stitch of the front and back needle. Knit these two sts together. *Knit the next two sts together in same manner. Pass the first st on the third needle over second st to BO. Rep from * until one st remains. Cut yarn and pull through.

TUBULAR CAST-ON

Using ribbing size needle and cotton scrap yarn, work chained cast-on (see Invisible Cast-On) for half the required total stitches plus 1. Switch to main yarn and knit one row (RS), purl one row, knit one row. With WS row facing, *purl first stitch, insert RH needle from top to bottom of first purl stitch in between scrap yarn. Place on RH needle going from front to back, and knit this stitch. Repeat from * ending with a purl stitch. Work k1, p1 ribbing.

TURKISH CAST-ON

This is my favorite cast-on when knitting toe-up socks with the magic loop method. There are other ways to do it, but when using magic loop you only need one set of needles.

Using circular needles, 32" or longer, hold both needles in your left hand with tips pointing left and place a slip knot on the bottom needle. Wrap half as many stitches as required around both needles from back to front.

While holding the needles as described above, grab the bottom of the two needles and pull it out till the loops are sitting on the cable and the top needles. Continue holding the top needle in you left hand and with your right hand grab the dangling needle that you just pulled out of the bottom. Knit the "loops" off the top needle

Flip your work so the cable is on top and the needle is on the bottom. Now push the top stitches off the cable onto the needle that is dangling. Pull out the bottom needle. You again will have stitches on the top needle and the bottom cable.

Holding the top needle in your left hand again, grab the bottom dangling needle with your right hand. The first loop on the top needle is the slipknot from your original cast-on. Drop this slipknot off the top needle and give it a tug. (This will get rid of the knot all together). Knit across rem stitches.

Continue as follows: Flip your work, push the top needle in, and pull the bottom needle out. Grab the bottom needle that you just pulled out and knit across the stitches. Repeat the above steps, pulling the first stitch tight, until you have created a small pouch. Your pattern should tell you how to increase for your toe.

BOOKSHELF ESSENTIALS

From technical resources to pure eye candy, these are some of my favorite knitting and fashion books.

VOGUE KNITTING: THE ULTIMATE KNITTING BOOK

Vogue Knitting Magazine Editors (Sixth&Spring Books)

It's the "go to" book for all your knitting questions.

DESIGNING KNITWEAR

Deborah Newton (Taunton)

The construction of a sweater finally clicked when I read this book.

KNITTING FROM THE TOP

Barbara G. Walker (Schoolhouse Press)

Create your own top-down patterns.

LUXURY KNITTING: THE ULTIMATE GUIDE TO EXQUISITE YARNS CASHMERE * MERINO * SILK

Linda Morse (Sixth&Spring Books)

This is a beautifully written guide on luxury fibers.

LOOP-D-LOOP: MORE THAN 40 NOVEL DESIGNS FOR KNITTERS

Teva Durham (Stewart, Tabori and Chang)

I'll always remember Teva as the person who taught me short rows. The book has gorgeous, unique designs.

BIG GIRL KNITS: 25 BIG, BOLD PROJECTS SHAPED FOR REAL WOMEN WITH REAL CURVES

Jillian Moreno and Amy Singer (Potter Craft)

The first four chapters, including how to adapt patterns to your shape, are a must for any knitter.

LUCY NEATBY'S COOL SOCKS WARM FEET

Lucy Neatby (Nimbus)

Not only does this book include unique sock patterns, but Neatby really explains the techniques behind them well.

VOGUE KNITTING STITCHIONARY SERIES: THE ULTIMATE STITCH DICTIONARY FROM THE EDITORS OF VOGUE KNITTING MAGAZINE

Trisha Malcolm (Sixth&Spring Books)

A great way to play with yarn. Use any of the stitches to create or adapt a pattern on your own.

THE ART OF KNITTING: INSPIRATIONAL STITCHES, TEXTURES, AND SURFACES

Francoise Tellier-Loumagne (Thames & Hudson)

This book was made to inspire your knitting and make you notice how the world around can be translated to color and textures in yarn.

KNITWEAR IN FASHION

Sandy Black (Thames & Hudson)

I love watching runway shows to pick up ideas for projects. I may not always apply them, but I love imagining. Keep this book nearby for the same feeling.

EXTREME BEAUTY: THE BODY TRANSFORMED (METROPOLITAN MUSEUM OF ART SERIES)

Harold Koda (Metropolitan Museum of Art)

The anthropologist in me loves this. A look at how body ideals and fashion change throughout time and cultures.

20TH CENTURY FASHION: 100 YEARS OF STYLE BY DECADE AND DESIGNER, IN ASSOCIATION WITH VOGUE

Linda Watson (Firefly Books)

Sketches, photographs, and reproductions from the pages of *Vogue*.

SAMPLE: 100 FASHION DESIGNERS - 010 CURATORS

Editors of Phaidon Press (Phaidon Press)

Fashion eye candy in a collage-like book, it's a collection of 100 young designers from around the world.

YARN SOURCES

BLUE SKY ALPACAS, INC
PO Box 88
Cedar, MN 55011
888.460.8862
www.blueskyalpacas.com

DEBBIE BLISS YARNS
Dist by Knitting Fever
PO Box 336
315 Bayview Ave.
Amityville, New York 11701
516.546.3600
www.knittingfever.com
www.debbieblissonline.com

ELSEBETH LAVOLD
Elizabeth Austen (see Debbie Bliss)
www.ingenkonst.se

FABLE HANDKNIT
5143 Tomken Road
Mississauga, Ontario
L4W 1P1 Canada
905.238.0388
www.fablehandknit.com

HABU TEXTILES
135 West 29th Street
Suite 804
New York, NY 10001
212.239.3546
www.habutextiles.com

KAALUND YARNS
Dist by Jumbuk Distribution
949.481.6696
www.kaalundyarns.com.au

LAINES DU NORD
Euro Yarn (see Debbie Bliss)

LOUISA HARDING YARNS
KFI (see Debbie Bliss)
www.louisaharding.co.uk

PEAR TREE
Jumbuk Distribution (see Kaalund)
www.peartreeproducts.com.au

PURE KNITS
www.pureknits.com

POSH YARN
www.poshyarn.co.uk

SHIBUIKNITS, LLC
1101 SW Alder
Portland, OR 97205
503.595.5898
www.shibuiknits.com

SUBLIME YARN
KFI (see Debbie Bliss)

TILLI TOMAS
Boston, MA
617.524.3330
www.tillitomas.com

YARNTINI
www.yarntini.net

ACKNOWLEDGMENTS

I owe thanks to those who kept me sane through this book's completion; I couldn't have done it without your help. Tom, who doesn't mind living in a home full of yarn or my constant talking about it. I promise a home-cooked meal soon! My parents, who gave me room to be whom or what I wanted. Sally Haggerty, for teaching me how to knit so many projects ago.

Stefanie Japel, who pushed me to take on this project and who's always a phone call or chat window away, no matter what else is going on. Stephanie Anesi, Maria Arguello, Leah Bear, Angela Fasudhani, Amy Sanders, and Joelene Wiggins—they were my sounding boards for anything, from the banal to the technical, and helped whenever they could.

All the designers who rose to the challenge and not only dealt with the crazy deadlines like champs, but sent in some of the most beautiful knitting I have seen. I'm so proud of you! The generous yarn companies who were sending bags of yarn around the world at the drop of a hat.

My editor, Wendy Gardner, for keeping me on track and showing patience at the same time. Wendy Preston, for taking on the challenge of pattern editing designs from such different styles. Holly Schmidt and Allan Penn, for approaching me with this idea and allowing me to add my own style.

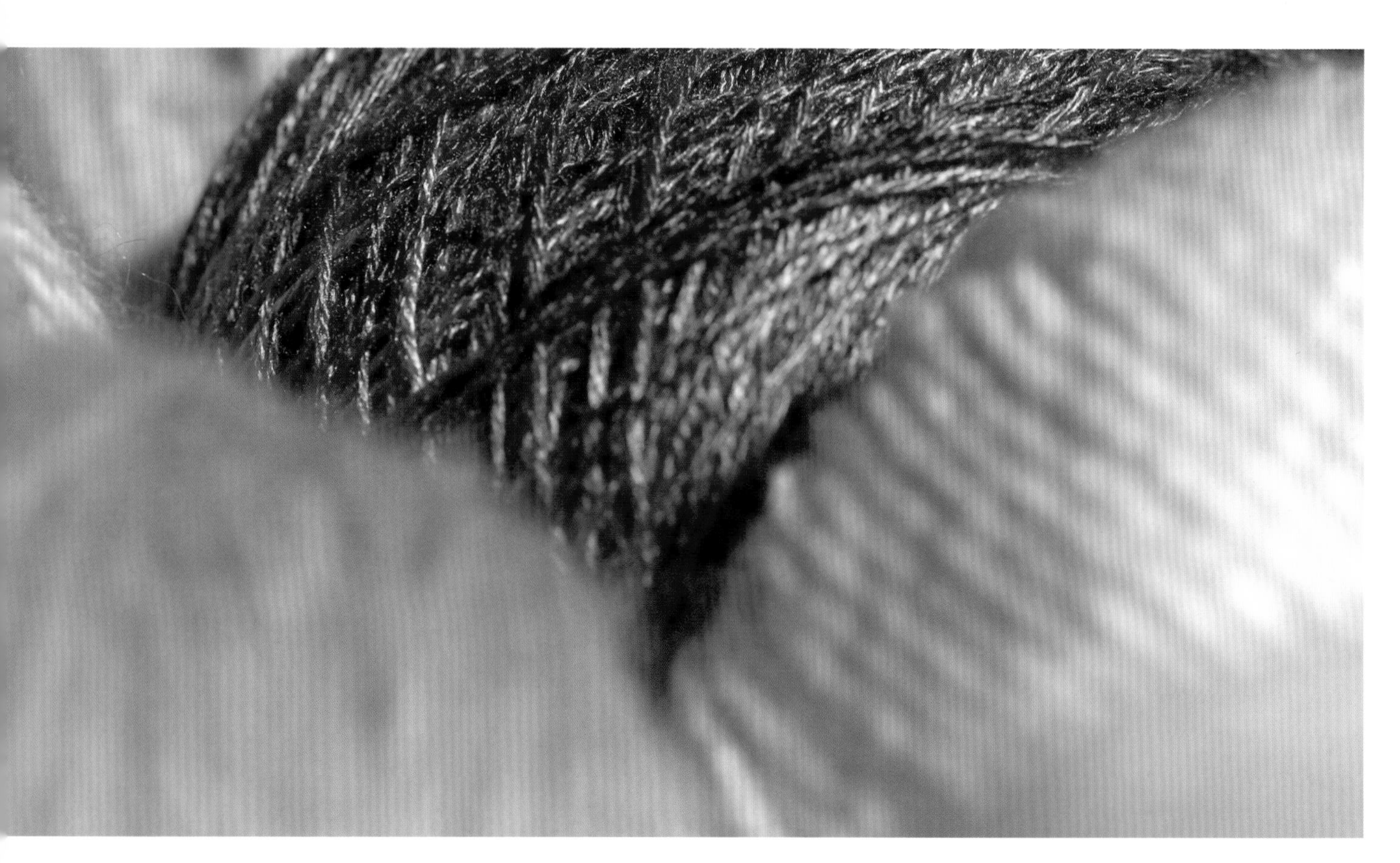

INDEX